WHAT'S THE BOOK ABOUT?

You were created for love! Here you will find the meaning of the love for which you were created. This book highlights the wholeness of relational love—God's love, parental love, covenant love, bridal love, intimacy of worship and prayer, persevering love, and love's great reward. All of this is wrapped-up in an intriguing love story of a quadriplegic Ph.D. and his highly intelligent bride, and their mutual passion for God and one another. The book impacts all ages and both genders!

What are people saying about the book? *Turn the page...*

COMMENTS BY YOUNG ADULTS WHO HAVE READ THE BOOK

A literary gem and timely message for this generation! — **Babett Mueller (Germany)**

I cannot speak too highly of this book! The story is raw and authentic! This is definitely on my top five favorite books. — **Katie Zyniewicz (Washington)**

This book is riveting! I give it five stars! — **Leah Johnson (Indiana)**

The book is so impacting! — **Andy Gloyd (Colorado)**

WOW. Inspiring! I felt so much love pouring out of the pages of this book. — **Skylar Moore (Kansas)**

An inspiring and provoking book on true intimacy of the heart! — **Amy Nelson (Texas)**

Wes' and Jane's love and passion for God's Word has inspired me to let the Word be my daily delight. — **Eileen Young (Connecticut)**

I could hardly put this book down! It greatly impacted my heart to read about the woman "behind the scene" of such an incredible man of God. — **Mallory Weyman (Ohio)**

This marriage displays many biblical values. I found the book to be healing. — **Aaron Moore (Colorado)**

This book is easy to pick up and hard to put down. The way God orchestrated these two lives together leaves an amazing impact. — **Charley Peters (California)**

An incredible story of God's beautiful leadership over two unique individuals! — **Anthony Sung (New Jersey)**

Reading this book is like watching a movie at times. — **Daniel Pitters (Michigan)**

This book describes a pure, tender, passionate, and truly life-giving love within marriage. — **Angelo J. Urbano (Connecticut)**

Jane's life of hiddenness and secret devotion in difficult circumstances moves one's heart. While reading this book, I could feel God's hand on me, increasing my hunger to be consumed by Jesus Christ. — **Rachelle Beauchamp (Arizona)**

An easy to read and hard to put down book! — **Katherine Green (Illinois)**

Jane's life gives me a grid for living a life of holiness in the context of love. — **Whitney Summerhays (Iowa)**

This beautiful book inspired me and gives me courage that I too can become a godly woman in this present evil age. — **Sara Marie Samsel (California)**

This book beautifully provides a biblical grid for understanding what true love and beauty is. — **Sarah Lee (Missouri)**

A treasury of living truth that reveals the potential we have to be the fragrance of Christ. — **Juliana Thompson (Ohio)**

Astutely written and beautiful! The book's pictures help the reader to identify with Wes and Jane in their life experiences. — **Lauren Beattie (Texas)**

This book provoked me to love with greater sacrifice, walk in greater integrity, revere God's Word more, and persevere even when the going gets tough. — **Corrie Magnuson (Missouri)**

A powerful testimony for our day when 50% of "Christian marriages" end in divorce! — **James Bricco (Illinois)**

The author skillfully unveils the intangible beauty that was in his wife. I plan to reread this book frequently! — **Luke Bloom (Kansas)**

I was eager at the end of each chapter to read what would happen next. The depths with which Wes knew Jane impacted my heart. — **Kellie Herrera (Missouri)**

The way Jane loved and served Wes, even in the midst of her own kidney troubles, is beyond beautiful! — **Paul Eastman (Florida)**

The servant heart of the people in Dr. Adams' life touched me! First, his parents amazed me how they gave so much of their lives to see him fulfill his calling. Second, the love of Jane for her quadriplegic husband is incredible! — **Jordan Zyniewicz (Washington)**

The commitment to love wholeheartedly as Jane did is rare in the earth! — **Trevor Carr (Michigan)**

This book gives the reader a sense of what a life of God-centered love looks like in marriage. — **David Yim (New Jersey)**

The Bride of Christ at the end of the age will have many of the same character qualities and virtues of Jane Adams. — **Valeria Rodriguez Caceres (Bolivia)**

This book really impacted me in the area of intimacy! It provoked me to set the bar higher in my relationship with God, with others in the body of Christ, and even my future marriage. — **Morgan Soeder (Ohio)**

I was challenged by Jane's servant heart and wholehearted love. Her desire for truth and integrity of heart and speech is amazing. — **Marjorie Misbeek (Arizona)**

COMMENTS BY SELECT FRIENDS OF WES & JANE

Read this book in one sitting. Deeply moving! — **Verena Dasser (Swiss Citizen)**

I was so moved by this story! For me it's a unique genre without precedent, with the exception of C.S. Lewis' book, A Grief Observed. Dr. Adams' account is actually richer, more miraculous than Lewis' book. — **Ken Robison, Author of Historical Letters in Cornell University Library (New York)**

The pages of this compelling book brought Jane alive again—her twinkled-eyed smile, her tenderhearted gentleness that made me feel at ease in her presence. Jane's story reminds me of the life and work of the Holy Spirit! — **Les Barker, Anglican Minister (Canada)**

This is a treasure! I laughed, cried, and was provoked in my passion for the Lord, and in my gratitude and love for my bridegroom, Les. — **Bonnie Barker, Chaplain (Canada)**

Fascinating reading! How special the depth of your love for Jane and her love for you! This book contains powerful insights into marriage and the Bridegroom King. — **Jane Norman, Children Evangelist (Missouri)**

Jane and Wes lived with us in Brazil for seven weeks. The book reveals much more about this unusual woman of God than I knew! — **Linda Stamps-Dinsmore, AG Missionary (Oklahoma City)**

This encourages faith! It describes an amazing, supernatural partnership of love and ministry that inspires awe of God's faithfulness. — **Rhonda Hughey, Director, Fusion Ministries (Kansas City)**

Jane was my friend since 4th grade. Words cannot describe the worth of this book! — **Maria Steiner (Phoenix, AZ)**

We wept as we read this excellent book! Describes Jane in a touching way. Expresses the same love that the Bridegroom has for His Bride! — **Rich & Dottie Kane, Healing Rooms Ministries (S. Florida)**

Devoured the book and pondered on it day and night. So inspiring! A GREAT BOOK! — **Catherine Shaver (Austin,TX)**

Jane, my friend for 19 years, truly had a servant's heart that exemplified Jesus' love. She and Wes danced seamlessly throughout those fleeting years. — **Dr. Todd Jones, DC (Missouri)**

Tenacious Love grips me at the core of my being! Such irresistible intimacy with Jesus! — **Rev. Charles Pickens, Nazarene Pastor & College Classmate of Wes Adams (Kansas)**

Every time I read Chapter 26, I tangibly feel the manifest presence of God's Love. — **Kellie Fenimore, Plumbline Ministries (Missouri)**

When reading Tenacious Love, I thought at first I was reading a book about Jane. As I read on, I thought, "No, this is a book about Jane and Wes." But as I continued, I discovered it is no more about Jane and Wes than the Bible is about Abraham and Moses, or Peter and Paul. Yes, these lives are shared in Scripture, but their lives simply reveal God's love as that of a bridegroom for a bride. Tenacious Love is a picture of the kind of love God has for us! — **Teckla Wilson (Oregon)**

TENACIOUS

LOVE

PORTRAIT OF A LIFE POURED OUT

JOHN WESLEY ADAMS

FOREWORD BY MIKE & DIANE BICKLE

Translations of the Bible used by permission

English Standard Version (ESV)
New American Standard Bible (NASB)
New International Version (NIV) 1984 Edition
New King James Version (NKJV)
New Living Translation (NLT)
New Revised Standard Version (NRSV)

Cover Design: Joshua Fenimore
Layout Design & Typesetting: Les Barker
Printed in the United States of America

Adams, John Wesley
Tenacious Love: Portrait of a Life Poured Out
ISBN# 978-1-530-97006-3
Published in Kansas City, Missouri (USA)

Dedicated

IN HONOR OF OUR PARENTS

J. KENNETH AND ELLA ADAMS

CLYDE AND MARCILE PETERSON

Who Blessed Us With Life & A Spiritual Heritage

Acknowledgements

❖ Deep appreciation goes to Kellie Fenimore, Jane's closest friend, who helped keep Jane's memory fresh in my heart during the months I was writing. Kellie, you're a precious daughter. Thank you!

❖ Much appreciation goes to Mike & Diane Bickle for reading the manuscript and for three decades of friendship.

❖ Thank you Jackie MacGirvin for your literary wisdom, strategic suggestions and invaluable contribution to the manuscript.

❖ Many thanks to Les and Bonnie Barker for their precious friendship and significant role in the interior design and appearance of the book.

❖ Thank you Dr. Denice Ross Haynes for your careful read and critique of the first draft. Your comments were brilliant!

❖ Thanks to Kara VanHover, my Class Assistant at the International House of Prayer University, to whom I dictated most of the book. Thanks to Kellie Fenimore and Lanelle Chase who also assisted.

❖ Thank you Wes and Carol Hall, Brian and Kellie Fenimore, Carol Hoffmeier and others who have helped recall Jane stories.

❖ Sincere thanks goes to three longtime friends, my faithful caregivers, whose daily physical assistance helped make this book possible—Ron Stewart, Kathy Butterbaugh and Kellie Fenimore.

❖ Finally, I'm so thankful for the extraordinary measure of God's presence and pleasure that I experienced while writing about Jane. His remarkable comfort made the book possible.

Contents

Foreword

R eading the story of Jane Adams, and her husband Wes, is like peering into the hearts of the great cloud of witnesses who have gone before us.

Who lives like this in today's modern, fast-paced world? Who suffers quietly, walks in humility and serves relentlessly—all at the same time? Who loves with a depth of love that holds steady in persecution, sickness and around-the-clock servitude?

Perhaps for a few years or maybe even for a decade someone may steward their heart to love like this. But who does it for a lifetime? Jane Adams did! She loved well for a lifetime.

Because the habit of Jane's life was to sit at Jesus' feet, her heart was continually enlarged! She took on His fragrance and character! She lived as Jesus lived—a meek and lowly servant for the sake of love.

Oh how Jane loved and cherished truth—"your Word O God is truth!" Jane was a doer of His Word. Jesus was the object of her affection and she was His.

She was consistently faithful and true as a wife, best friend, partner and, yes, caregiver to Wes, her quadriplegic husband for 30 years. The fire of her love for Jesus was given expression day in and day out, night after night, year after year as she bestowed that passion and tender care upon Wes. What a champion of love she was!

Jane's tenacious love raises the bar for us all, but also gives us hope. Her life will inspire you to be filled with the love of God and to let that love rule your heart, your words and your actions in all your relationships.

Her love was a gift to Wes and to all of us who seek to love truer, deeper and longer in humility.

Mike and Diane Bickle
International House of Prayer of Kansas City
Director and Wife

Special Tribute

Words fail to capture the place Jane has in our hearts! She was a delightful bundle of paradoxes. In my course on C. S. Lewis, it was clear that Jane had discovered a kindred spirit in Lewis. Like Lewis, Jane brought a razor sharp logic to everything. And yet Jane was also a mystic in many ways. She could offer the most logical interpretations of the dreams God gave her. For Jane, the uniting of faith and reason was effortless.

Jane was the most serious and earnest person one could meet; yet in a split-second she could be as playful as a child. Although both Wes and I had Jane as a student, I think we both knew we had met our match intellectually. But Jane was truly humble and saw all learning as a way of getting at the truth, not a means of self-promotion.

Over the years, Teckla and I have often commented that there are few people we have enjoyed more than Jane: her humor and genuineness always refreshed our spirits. She didn't have a "religious" bone in her body. Her ability to simply be what God made her gave everyone around her permission to be themselves.

At the very end of Tolkien's *Lord of the Rings,* Sam has to say a final goodbye to Frodo with whom he has gone through so much. Tolkien describes him as "filled with a sadness that was yet blessed and without bitterness." This describes many parts of *Tenacious Love.* It is a skillfully crafted tribute to an amazing woman, wife and friend.

It is to Jane's credit that this book tells us as much about God's love for us, as her unrelenting love of Wes. This book should give hope to all who seek God's grace in impossible circumstances. It is the story of life lived with holy excellence.

Professor Mark Wilson
Myrtle Beach, Oregon
Jane's College Professor on C. S. Lewis

Wes and Jane Adams

Introduction
Power Of A Righteous Life

A woman who fears the Lord will be greatly praised.

Proverbs 31:30 NLT

L ove in the Song of Songs is described as a tenacious flame that many waters cannot quench or extinguish. The Shulamite describes to her beloved the tenaciousness of the flame of love: *"Place me like a seal over your heart, like a seal on your arm; for love is as strong as death, its jealousy unyielding as the grave. It burns like blazing fire, like a **mighty flame**. Many waters cannot quench love; rivers cannot wash it away."¹*

You are about to read of the humble life of a most remarkable bride. In her union with God, in her tenacious love, and in her experience of the "dark night of the soul," Jane was like her Lord.

You probably never had opportunity to know Jane and be enriched by her. She was a hidden jewel. This book is your opportunity. Scripture says a woman who truly fears God will be greatly praised. Though not perfect, none of us are, Jane loved and feared God more deeply than any woman I have ever known.

This is not a romance book, though it is indeed a true love story. The book reveals the many facets of love's flame and illustrates that authentic spirituality is indeed possible in a 21st Century Western nation.

Your heart will be melted by this story of a faithful bride who poured out her life because of love. At times you will laugh, at other times you may cry, but at all times you will be edified.

Who was Jane Adams? Why this book about her? Because God wants the fragrance of Jesus in her righteous life, previously hidden from public view, to bless others. Her life will inspire you to give more of yourself to God.

In these pages you'll learn how creative God can be in bringing a couple together for His purpose. Jane and I were an unlikely match—she a brainy WHO'S WHO female college student and me a Ph.D. college professor.

In these pages you'll see what a human picture of tenacious love looks like. *Tenacious* means "keeping a firm hold; refusing to let go or give up; strongly persistent." You'll see what a young bride's love for God and her husband looks like after decades of marriage and adversity.

In Jane you'll gain an enlarged understanding of what the word faithful means. *Faithful* (Gk. *pistos*) means to be "full of faith" (Gk. *pistis*). Jane was a faith-filled person, steadfast and trustworthy. She modeled follow-through on promises, always keeping her word in little ways and big.

As a quadriplegic, totally confined to a wheelchair since age 16, I've often experienced God's tenacious love and faithfulness. I've also seen them expressed brilliantly and consistently in Jane. Yet always it was His steadfast love and faithfulness that went before and made it all possible. Had God not been there, the outcome would have been different.

> *"Not to us, O Lord, not to us,*
> *but to your name goes all the glory*
> *for your unfailing love and faithfulness."*
> *(Ps. 115:1 NLT)*

---

[1] Song of Songs 8:6, 7a - NIV 1984

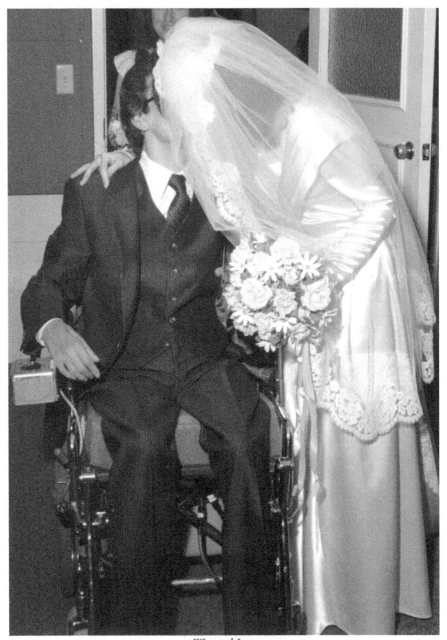

Wes and Jane
Wedding Kiss

1

The Flame

*Set me as a seal upon your heart...for love is strong as death.
Its flashes are flashes of fire, the very flame of the Lord.*

Song of Songs 8:6 ESV

You were created for love! Love is transformational! True love originates with God and is *"the very flame of the Lord."*[1] Love comes from God, is expressed to and through humans, and then returns back to God. Love's flame will burn on and on forever because it is the Lord's flame.

It was a monumental love-moment when Jane, my 23-year old bride, said to me, her quadriplegic bridegroom, "I do!" She knew and I knew that our love for one another, like flashes of fire, was now being fused as a flame into a life-time covenant of love and marriage.

On an autumn evening in 2010, I faced our love-bond's most difficult moment. Thirty years had passed as I pulled my specially equipped van into the driveway and maneuvered my power chair into the house. Our dog, Duke,[2] enthusiastically greeted me at the door. I petted his head and rolled into the living room where my sweetheart sat in a recliner. I was concerned. I could tell she wasn't doing well.

The kidney transplant six weeks previously had gone remarkably well. The doctors had assured us that this new young kidney was a great match and they were even decreasing her medicine. Jane's normally high blood pressure had come down, a good sign, but tonight it was too low and her heart rate was too high. Kathy, one of our roomers and caregivers, had been helping Jane all evening while I had been at the International House of Prayer.

Kathy turned to me, "She's been vomiting and she's running a temperature."

I asked Jane some questions and had her do a blood pressure reading. It was alarmingly low, especially for her. The heart rate was alarmingly high—racing. I called Jane's transplant nurse, but her advice was simply, "Just monitor it."

Two days before, on Friday, had been Jane's best day in a long time. She was happy, her countenance was glowing, and she was generally vibrant and full of life. On Saturday she hadn't felt quite as well. And Sunday was definitely an off day.

About 10:00 P.M., over Jane's objections, I called 911 and requested an ambulance. I didn't want to take a chance with her heart.

Soon lights were flashing in front of our house. The confidence and competence of the EMTs[3] had a calming effect on Jane. I prayed as I watched them wheel her into the back of the big emergency vehicle. Kathy rode with her. I followed in my wheelchair-equipped van, praying all the way to the hospital, about a 20-minute drive.

We were in the ER[4] by 11:00 P.M. I knew we were not alone in this crisis. My trust was foremost in God. But I also felt better knowing that Jane could have her problem assessed, monitored, and resolved by medical professionals. After all, it was nothing short of a miracle that she had received a perfect kidney transplant just in time a few weeks before and was rapidly recovering.

The ER was chilly. I knew Jane would be cold, so I requested blankets. Kathy helped cover her while the doctor read her med records, including her recent transplant history.

He ordered IV's and antibiotics. Jane's heart continued to race. The rate was in the 140s. Though she was well hydrated and receiving medical attention, her heart rate wasn't coming down. The doctor phoned Jane's kidney specialist and a cardiologist, requesting they come to the hospital. He told me, "If she weren't a woman, I would say she was having a heart attack."

A nurse, the ER doctor, Kathy, and I were around Jane's bed when I saw her grimace and grip the side rail to sit up.

I asked, "Jane, what's going on?"

"I don't know." Those were her last words as she fell back on the bed and the monitor flat lined.

The room exploded into a flurry of activity. The doctor immediately put an oxygen mask on Jane and began CPR. Respiratory therapists came quickly with their equipment. I looked at her and the monitor in horror—Jane's heart wasn't responding.

Kathy and I were ushered into the hall. I paced and prayed. My heart was resisting the fear that was trying to choke me. The spiritual atmosphere was oppressive. After some time, the doctor came to me. His remarks were brief. "It looks very grim. We're doing all we can."

---

[1] *Song of Songs 8:6 ESV*

[2] *Duke is a Border Collie and Australian Kelpie mix, which Jane and I obtained as a six-week old puppy not long after moving back from England. The bond between Jane and Duke was extraordinary.*

[3] *Emergency Medical Technicians*

[4] *Emergency Room*

Jane at 3 years, her parents and Don

Jane, age 6, and Don her brother

2

Bright

What will this child turn out to be?

Luke 1:66 NLT

Jane was bright and precocious as a child. She memorized a poem of 36 lines in its entirety at the age of three. Her brightness was evident in the first grade. Her mother conferred with Jane's teacher near the end of the school year. Her teacher remarked, "Mrs. Peterson, Jane is ready for the second grade. In fact, she could probably handle the third grade." Then she added, "Actually Jane could handle anything she wants to do."

What an amazing testimony from Jane's first grade teacher, quite different from my first grade teacher's communication with my parents. "Wesley does not pay attention in class, disturbs others, and needs help reading."

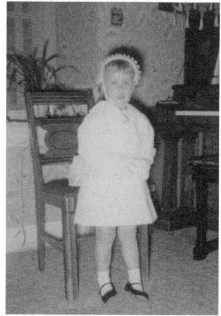

Jane, age 3

Jane's Parents

Jane's parents were gifted people. Her mother, a highly gifted pianist, played for adult worship services at age eight. Marcile is still, in her eighties, one of the most skilled pianists I know when it comes to hymns, gospel music and playing by ear. Her mother is a prolific reader.

Her father had a genius level intelligence. The U.S. Army drafted him at age 23, two months after Pearl Harbor. He served during World War II on the front lines as a shortwave radio operator in England and Europe. His life was in constant peril, including the Normandy invasion, the brutal Battle of the Bulge and the final march to Berlin that forced Hitler's army to surrender.

After Clyde finished his faithful military service for his country and returned to Kansas, he worked for the Union Pacific Railroad until retirement. The last 17 years with Union Pacific were spent as depot agent at Wamego, Kansas.[1] This sleepy little town is where Jane grew up from age two until she went to college and married her favorite professor.

Jane's childhood and youth were a picture of stability. She lived in the same house from age three, went to the same church, and went through the same public school system from preschool through high school.

Learning Adventures

During her childhood and youth, Jane—with her parents and older brother, Don—travelled for two weeks every summer on vacation. Each year they went to a new location in the United States. Travel can be educational; Jane's summers were an enjoyable form of education.

In the classroom, Jane was a young scholar from the beginning. As a child, she was a prolific reader, an exceptional speller and full of factual knowledge. More than once at a young age, she would raise her hand in class and correct her teacher's wrong pronunciation of a word or call attention to a factual error in class content.

Jane excelled in all 12 grades and graduated from high school as valedictorian of her class. She was given the most elite academic scholarship available at her Christian College.

Again Jane excelled academically and made all A's. She not only graduated as valedictorian of her university senior class, but also received the American Heritage Award, the highest non-academic award given to one male and one female graduating senior at Commencement.

The Bible

At a young age, Jane's love for God included precise attention to the Holy Scriptures. She read her Bible carefully during childhood and believed it was God's Word. As a small girl she would sit in adult preaching services, following along in her Bible, always puzzled when the preacher was inaccurate about Bible facts or statements in his message. Later, as an adult, Jane was always irritated when a preacher would mishandle or manipulate the biblical text in any way.

In her teens, Jane and her parents visited relatives in western Kansas. On Sunday her family went to church together. Although Jane knew no one, she went to the Sunday school class for her age. The lesson that day was from I Timothy. The teacher said Timothy wrote the book. Jane knew that was not true, but checked to make sure. She opened her Bible and there at its beginning were the words, "The Epistle of Paul to Timothy."

She called the teacher's attention to the fact that the book was *to* Timothy, not *by* Timothy. The teacher refused to back down. Jane then read out loud the first two verses of the book: "Paul, an apostle of Jesus Christ,... to Timothy, a true son in the faith."[2] Jane said, "This was written *by* Paul to his spiritual son, Timothy." The teacher again responded, "No, it was written by Timothy."

At that point, Jane closed her Bible and knew first hand that those in positions of authority can be very wrong. Her view of Sunday school teachers was never quite the same after that. From a young age, Jane exhibited traits that would make her an excellent helpmate for a college Bible professor.

As a young adult, Jane was working on her M.A. degree in Classics at the University of Kansas. Her professor, in a course on Greek Mythology, made a comment about how late a particular New Testament book of the Bible was written, dating its origin in the second century. He added that the book was therefore inaccurate.

Jane raised her hand. It was probably the first time a student challenged his statement. "My husband is a New Testament scholar, and he says this was written in the first century." The professor made some rude, smart aleck remark and blew off her comment as being misinformed.

After Jane came home, she told me about her professor's comments. I probably aggravated the situation by saying, "Jane, this guy doesn't know what he is talking about. Even the most liberal biblical scholars do not date the origin of that New Testament book in the second century."

At this point, Jane knew firsthand there are not only Sunday School teachers, but also university professors who don't know what they're talking about. Needless to say, Jane did not trust that professor thereafter.

The psalmist testifies that God has exalted, above all things, His name and His Word.[3] Imagine the delight this must have given her heavenly Father as Jane boldly embraced His Word publicly in a state university. She was expressing the same kind of love the Father looks for in the faithful Bride, whom He will present to His Son at the end of the age.

---

[1] *Wamego was then a small farming community of 2,500 people in northeast Kansas.*

[2] *1 Tim. 1:1-2*

[3] *Ps. 138:2 ESV*

Wes With His Parents
Wes, Age Two

Wes With His Parents & Sister, Eileen
Wes, Age 14 (barely)

3

Night Of Regret

Do not remember the rebellious sins of my youth.
Remember me in the light of your unfailing love,
for you are merciful, O Lord.

Psalm 25:7 NLT

J ane and I grew up in the same denomination. In many ways our backgrounds were similar; in other ways they were quite different. My parents met at Pasadena College[1] and married in their mid-thirties. A year later I was born. The Lord prompted them to name me John Wesley, after the great 18th century evangelist and revivalist in England. They believed from the beginning that God's hand was on me to preach the gospel and that He had a special destiny for my life.

Both my father and mother were capable preachers, pastoring a small church in Wyoming during their first year of marriage. I was dedicated to the Lord as a baby by a missionary from Japan who prophesied to my mother, "Your son will need you more when he is 17 than he does now." My mother wondered, *"How can a son need a mother more at 17 than as an infant?"* The prophecy proved to be shockingly accurate.

Sixteen

Fast-forward 16 years to Oklahoma. The night of the El Reno High School prom was the occasion of my personal nightmare. My girlfriend was on the banquet program as a singer. Afterwards, instead of staying for the prom, we double dated with church friends to an amusement park. About 11:30 P.M., I took Janice home, and met some of my unsaved buddies for a night of partying.

I was in a place of teenage rebellion. That was the only night in my entire life I was ever drunk. Our car wreck that night was totally unnecessary! It happened early in the morning hours as a direct result of alcohol. Of the five boys in the car, I was the only person seriously injured, and the only one raised in a clearly Christian home. I was asleep in the back seat when the wreck occurred.

Although we had a designated driver who was sober, the car owner's son, who had been drinking, forcefully demanded to drive. Larry drove recklessly, spinning the car in circles on the highway.

At that point another intoxicated passenger insisted on having his turn at the wheel. Dennis attempted to do the same kind of spinning but ended up rolling the car. One by one the four other guys crawled from the mangled car with cuts, bruises, and minor injuries. When it was my turn to crawl out, I realized I could not move my body.

We later learned my neck had been broken and spinal cord damaged, paralyzing me instantly from the chest down, shortly before my 17th birthday. Larry, who had taken the car without his father's permission, panicked and pulled the seats out so that the boys could pull me out of the wreckage. They laid me beside the highway on a cold May 17th morning. An ambulance was called and we all waited. I don't know how long I lay there, but long enough to get pneumonia before the ambulance arrived.

Everything about this picture was wrong. I was uncovered spiritually because of my teenage rebellion. The car was taken against the wishes of Larry's father. Alcohol, which dulls the mind, causes 16-year-old boys to be more stupid and reckless than normal. My own intoxication in the back seat placed me in the vulnerable situation that unfolded. That one night of foolish fun caused me years of remorse, regret and incalculable suffering. Such is the ugly story of sin and rebellion.

Only two of the four boys involved in the accident continued their friendship with me for a time. Even more sadly, none of the four—to my knowledge—have become Christians. Twenty-five years later, I wrote a letter to all four guys, explaining the goodness of God in my life subsequent to that disastrous night. I assured them that I held no grudge against any of them for the outcome.

What became of them? Three grew up to have much misery in their lives. Ironically I, who seemed to have incurred the worst "fate", have clearly had the most meaningful and happy life because of Jesus Christ. Such is the power of redeeming love!

Encounter

My mother came directly to my side after receiving the phone call. My father, being at work, came later. For 36 hours it was uncertain whether I would live.

I was first taken to the closest community hospital, and then sent by ambulance to a large hospital in Oklahoma City, ironically named Wesley Hospital. I remained semi-unconscious. My mother did a non-stop prayer vigil. Doctors and nurses encouraged her to take a break, eat and get some sleep, but she refused to leave my side even for 15 minutes.

At one point, while in intercession, she saw demons come to the foot of my bed, sneering and mocking, "We've come to take him away."

My mother had never seen demons before or since. She had never attended a spiritual warfare conference or seminar. Nonetheless the Holy Spirit led and empowered her to resist them in the name of Jesus and to plead His blood over my life. The demons backed down and disappeared.

Mom continued to pray, 36 hours total, refusing to leave my side. The breakthrough moment came when the Lord brought to her mind the words of a hymn—

My faith looks up to Thee,
Thou Lamb of Calvary, Savior divine!
Now hear me while I pray,
take all my guilt away,
O let me from this day be wholly Thine!

May Thy rich grace impart
Strength to my fainting heart, my zeal inspire!
As Thou hast died for me,
O may my love to Thee,
Pure, warm, and changeless be, a living fire!

At the end of her 36-hour vigil, I came out of my near unconsciousness, became fully alert and began breathing normally. My mother then shared with me, best she could, what had happened and that I was paralyzed. In that somber moment, she urged me to make my peace with God.

Immediately, I confessed my sin of rebellion—to God and to my parents, asking Him and them to forgive me. When I did, my hospital cubicle was illumined by the presence of Jesus as He gave me the biggest kiss of forgiveness. He so touched my heart with His amazing love, I began to worship Him—and sing aloud:

> *Amazing Grace, how sweet the sound,*
> *That saved a wretch like me*
> *I once was lost but now am found,*
> *Was blind, but now, I see.*[2]

These words expressed the burning reality of the encounter I was having with Jesus. I was completely oblivious to the five other patients and their guests as I sang aloud there in the hospital ward.

Physical Rehabilitation

This divine moment carried me through the days ahead. For six weeks, I lay on a Stryker Frame[3] unable to move, my head in traction secured by screws drilled into my skull. No TV or radio were provided. I was fed by nurses but otherwise alone. I had plenty of time to reflect about what had happened to me.

The first days and weeks of trauma, and the next 18 months of rehabilitation, were exceedingly difficult! Nevertheless, doctors and nurses remarked to my parents what an unusual patient I was, given my situation.

There was an explanation! Although I couldn't articulate it at the time, my Jesus-encounter and God's presence were supernaturally sustaining me. Doctors, nurses and others could see it!

I thought at the time I was experiencing normal Christianity. Not until a few years later did I realize the measure of God's presence I experienced in my fiery ordeal was exceptional. It was indeed normal in the book of Acts, but typically not normal in the contemporary Western church.

Divine Compass

Like the cross and tragic death of Jesus, I came to believe my accident was both a setup of the devil seeking to destroy my life but, at the same time, a severe mercy of God seeking to redeem my life. Without violating my free will, God mercifully interrupted my headlong plunge toward a wasted life and ultimately hell. As the psalmist said, *"Before I was afflicted I went astray, but now I obey your word. You are good, and what you do is good."*[4] Only God can fully transform a tragedy into a triumph that redeems, glorifies Him and blesses others.

After 18 long months of hospitalization and physical rehabilitation, I came home to live with my parents and sister, Eileen, who was two years younger. It was time to face the future as a greatly disabled paralytic.

A few weeks after my final discharge from physical rehabilitation, God spoke clearly to me through what became a life-verse for my journey:

Trust in the LORD with all your heart, and lean not on your own understanding. In all your ways acknowledge Him, and He shall direct your paths.[5]

My first challenge in trusting God was to finish high school in the classroom with my peers, rather than being taught in isolation at my house. I knew the only way to overcome my being severely self-conscious, as a former athlete now confined to a wheelchair, was to return to the classroom.

My parents had moved 20 miles from El Reno to Bethany, Oklahoma. The house they rented was one mile from Bethany High School. My father worked a daytime job; my mother and sister were unable to lift me in and out of a car. There was no transport available to get me to the high school and back. "Lord," I prayed, "will you make a way?"

Shortly after praying, a free-advertising paper was left at our front door. It listed items for sale and houses for rent. I had never before looked at it, but picked it up and saw that there was a house for rent on the corner directly across from the high school.

When my father returned from work, he and my mother hurried to see it. When they arrived, however, the house had just been rented. But the new renters had lived next door and that house was now available.

Miracle House for Schooling

My parents seized this opportunity! Within a month we moved literally right across the street from my classes. My sister could push me in a manual wheelchair to school where I attended classes with my peers. The Lord had answered my specific request in a very short time. He made it possible for me to join classmates for the final semester of my senior year.

Wes in a manual wheel chair as a college freshman being pulled up a long flight of stairs to his class

It's amazing how God, in His wisdom, is able to work many things together at once for our good when we love and trust Him. This house across the street from Bethany High School was also God's provision for my next five years. Providentially, this same house was located just two blocks from Bethany Nazarene College[6] the college from which I would obtain B.A. and M.A. degrees. The college campus was older and there were no cutouts at curbs for wheelchairs. The building entrances in 1960 all had stairs to get to classrooms (picture). But I permitted no kind of obstacle, physical or otherwise, to deter me from pursuing God's call. The convenient location of my house to BNC was such that college friends and classmates could push me in my manual wheelchair from my house to college classrooms without the labor of lifting me in and out of an automobile for transport. I did this in all kinds of weather for five years.

Before getting back to Jane's story, you will be best prepared to understand her unusual life if you understand the man she married and the important preparation that preceded our meeting.

---

[1] Located in Pasadena, California

[2] "Amazing Grace" by John Newton, written in 1779 while an Anglican vicar at a small church in Olney, England.

[3] A metal frame designed to place the neck in traction, but to be able to swivel the patient every two hours into two positions: back or stomach. Later model Stryker Frames are capable of other degrees of position.

[4] Psalm 119:67-68a NIV

[5] Proverbs 3:5-6 NKJV

[6] Now Southern Nazarene University

Wes At Gaylord, Kansas
Age 28

4

God Is A Good Leader

I am the Lord your God, who teaches you what is best for you, who directs you in the way you should go.

Isaiah 48:17 NIV

Planning for my vocational future as a quadriplegic was an important part of my post-high school preparation. Oklahoma assisted me through an agency called Oklahoma Vocational Rehabilitation Services (VR). This state agency gave me aptitude exams and counseling concerning a future vocational choice. The goal was to train me to be gainfully employed as a paralytic.

My VR counselor recommended that I enroll as a pre-law major. VR believed my profile fit that of a lawyer, a vocation I could also do as a paralytic. Also, conventional wisdom said I was going to need a large income to hire caregivers and pay my expenses as a quad.

Pre-Law Major

I enrolled in college as a history and pre-law major. But in October my freshman year, God began to speak to me on my bed at night about surrendering my life to Him for the work of ministry. Like Moses at the burning bush, I had many reasons why this was not a good idea and why I was incapable of fulfilling His call. "Lord," I argued, "there are many young men on campus with good legs and hands. Why not ask one of them?"

Over the course of several weeks, God continued to speak to me during the night hours. One by one He listened to my list of reservations. *How would I ever make enough income in the ministry to support myself? What church would want a pastor confined to a wheelchair with my level of paralysis?* I was unable to foresee how this could possibly work.

God was patient in dealing with my fears and objections. However, after days and weeks, I knew that if I continued to resist Him, I would be in rebellion. And I didn't want to go there again!

Finally, by faith, I fully surrendered my will and my future to Him completely. The lyrics of the hymn, *"I Surrender All,"*[1] describe well what transpired in my heart:

1. *All To Jesus I Surrender*
   All To Him I Freely Give
   I Will Ever Love And Trust Him
   In His Presence Daily Live.

   > *Chorus: All To Jesus I Surrender,*
   > *Humbly At His Feet I Bow*
   > *Worldly Pleasures All Forsaken*
   > *Take Me Jesus, Take Me Now.*

2. *All To Jesus I Surrender*
   Make Me Savior Wholly Thine
   Let Me Feel The Holy Spirit
   Truly Know That Thou Are Mine.

3. *All To Jesus I Surrender,*
   Lord I Give Myself To Thee
   Fill Me With Thy Love And Power
   Let Thy Blessing Fall On Me.

When I fully surrendered to God and leaned into His calling, great peace filled my heart. I had a deep assurance that if I did my part in preparation, He would do His part in opening doors and using me in the ministry.

Bible and Theology

Having been captured by God, I immediately changed my major to biblical and theological studies. My VR counselor was indignant. He felt

Oklahoma's VR tuition money would be wasted. But after my God encounter and call, I was resolved and never looked back.

God declares, and His Word is true, *"Cursed is the one who trusts in man.... Blessed is the man who trusts in the LORD, whose confidence is in him."*[2]

I threw myself into my college studies with great earnestness. I had wasted my first three years in high school and failed to develop good study habits. Consequently, I was at a great disadvantage my freshman year. I had to work doubly hard to develop study habits and to discipline my wandering mind when studying. My first year, I took general courses required for a Bachelor of Arts degree.

My sophomore year I enrolled in the kind of courses that most interested me. Since being captured by God, what interested me most were classes like Beginning Greek, Church History, Book of Acts, and Systematic Theology. I excelled in each of these courses! This was quite a turnaround from my high school junior year when I almost flunked all of my classes. What a difference God makes in our desires and motivations when He transforms us by His majestic ownership!

After encountering Jesus in the hospital, literally everything about my life changed. I longed to read, study and grow in knowledge and truth. I was highly motivated! After four years, I graduated with a B.A. in Religion and a 3.62 Grade Point Average.

Graduate Degrees

After college, I inquired of the Lord, "What do I do now?" His reply? "Stay in college and get an M.A. degree in Biblical and Theological Studies." This degree required 30 classroom hours plus a M.A. Thesis. I completed this in one year by beginning summer school immediately after college graduation and using the next summer to write my 140-page thesis. God stood with me in this, and I graduated with straight A's.

After the M.A. degree, I inquired of the Lord again, "What do I do now?" His reply? "Go to seminary." I was not so sure about this answer. I told no one and prayed about it a great deal. One day my father unexpectedly said, "I think you're supposed to go to seminary. Your mother and I are willing to sell our house and move with you to Kansas City so that you can attend Nazarene Theological Seminary, if that's what you want."

I knew the Lord had confirmed His word through my father. After completing my M.A. Thesis, my parents and I moved to Kansas City. The seminary M.Div. degree was a three-year graduate program, designed to prepare aspiring young ministers to be pastors and leaders. The three-year study was a grind. As with my previous degree programs, however, the Lord stood beside me and enabled me to excel. Three years later I graduated with a 3.96 GPA, ranking second in my graduating class.

Wilderness Years

After the M.Div. degree, I inquired of the Lord, "What do I do next?" There was only silence. I wanted to travel as an evangelist, but that was impossible. The next two years I spent in a small rural town in north-central Kansas, ministering along side my father in a very small church.

I later came to understand this was exactly what I needed. But at the time, I felt abandoned by God. My three degrees seemed for nothing! My flesh was being crucified and I was dying! I struggled with serious doubts about my future. These were my wilderness years! During them I had to trust God at a new level.

I had to learn an important lesson in a new way. It was necessary for me again to let go of the past and embrace the future. The past is the past because it is past. Let go of the past mentally and emotionally. Don't hang onto it. Live in the present! And embrace the future! Trying to hang onto the past is a hindrance to going forward in the present and hearing God's heartbeat for the future.

The contrasts between my lifestyle the previous three years and my two wilderness years were dramatic. Previously, I lived in Kansas City, a big metropolis; the wilderness years were in Gaylord, a tiny rural town of 300 people. The local farmers were in sharp contrast to my intellectual seminary professors and classmates. The pace of my seminary years was fast; the pace of my two wilderness years was exceedingly slow.

I came to Gaylord, Kansas highly educated in Bible and Theology. My first assignment was teaching a small junior and senior high Sunday School class. That was hard on my ego, but exactly what my ego needed.

God was personally mentoring me these two years in humility and faith. The slower pace of life (no TV, no smart phone, no laptop or computer of any kind, no powerchair & van, etc.) gave me much time for reflection, reading, developing new life interests, spending more time with God in His Word and in prayer, and learning to love ordinary people.

After a transition of six months, I was appointed interim pastor for one year in a nearby community where I preached in morning and evening Sunday services every week. I also began to receive invitations to hold special services in churches around the area. These two wilderness years were an important education of a different kind, further preparing me for the future.

New Direction

Near the end of my wilderness season, God began to speak to me about a doctoral degree. This seemed preposterous! Impossible! Physically, financially and in other ways impossible! It was as impossible as when the Lord called me to preach the gospel my first semester in college. God continued to probe me.

I tentatively decided in early spring to investigate some universities and seminaries with doctoral programs in Biblical and Theological Studies. Most had already filled their student quota for that autumn. I would have to wait a year and a half before beginning my Ph.D. studies.

When the dust settled, the university, location and degree program that most appealed to me was Baylor University. They still had an opening in the fall. But my physical and financial limitations still made this seem like an impossible road to travel.

I had many questions and hesitations. Hadn't I already accomplished more than anyone could possibly expect from a quadriplegic? Did I have the energy and capability that completing a Ph.D. would require? Furthermore, my parents were now in their mid-sixties. How could I possibly expect them to move and assist me through another grinding educational endeavor? These questions seemed overwhelming. So I simply committed the whole thing back to God, believing that if He were initiating this, He would somehow make it possible.

I was amazed when, a few months later, my father approached me with a proposal. "I think you should earn a Ph.D. Your mother and I will move with you and help just like before." At that point, I knew in my heart that God was saying, *"This is the way, walk in it."*[3] My doubts and reservations suddenly seemed less overwhelming.

The Test of Adversity

My parents and I were severely tested in this new direction. Shortly before our move, my father was hospitalized with a shoulder problem. During the journey from Gaylord to Waco[4], my mother had a physical collapse from which it took months to recover.

I was severely attacked in my thoughts and emotions. I feared that carnal ambition had deceived me, and my parents were now suffering as a result. Everything about the move was difficult and discouraging, but the Lord sustained all three of us through the storm. The sun did shine again!

When I arrived at Baylor, the Jesus People Revival was gaining a presence on university campuses nationwide. It was so at Baylor and in some Waco churches. I had long prayed for revival and this was a little taste. My spirit was enlivened, my mind was sharpened, my energy increased and my love for people grew steadily.

Simultaneous with my academic studies, I had the privilege of teaching a young-adult class on Sundays and a home group during the week. Both were stimulating and enabled me to put into practice what I was learning in my studies, thus enhancing my abilities in both spheres.

My years at Baylor were a huge growing curve. An anointing to teach increased and doors for teaching opened. God used all this to motivate me in my doctoral studies and to dream about becoming a college professor in New Testament Studies.

Financial Mountain

There was a towering mountain in front of me. How do I pay for such an expensive degree program when there is no money in my bank account? None! Is it really true that when "God guides, God provides"? I believed so, but now I had to learn if it were true.

From the beginning, my Baylor Ph.D. seemed financially impossible. Before moving to Waco, God opened doors for speaking that brought extra money for my moving expenses. This strengthened my faith for a financial miracle.

The Lord impressed several different people to give me monetary gifts; this too encouraged me to trust Him. When it came time to move from Kansas to Texas, I had just enough money to make the move, pay the first month's rent and enroll for one course at Baylor. Then my money was completely depleted.

What next? Did He not promise that if I did my part, He would do His part and make my path straight? I again affirmed my trust in His leadership.

Supernatural provision then began to unfold. I received a phone call from El Reno; it was the father of the young man with whom I had double dated the night before my accident. He had heard I was starting doctoral studies and offered to pay for my textbooks and typing costs, both being considerable expenses.

Next, I received a letter from Texas Vocational Rehabilitation Services inviting me to come to their office for a consultation. Because my experience with VR in Oklahoma was not good after I changed my major to Bible, I assumed it would be futile to contact the VR in Texas. When I received a second letter, I asked my father to take me.

My counselor was a good Southern Baptist and was excited for me. He asked, "Why did you wait so long? Didn't you know that Texas VR will pay your full tuition for the Ph.D.?" That was a Wow moment! I could hardly believe my ears. In Oklahoma they would not pay a dime on graduate degrees at a private university.

Still another provision occurred. For the first time, Social Security provided me with a monthly check to help cover basic living expenses as a student.

Can God be trusted as a Leader? From the time I fully surrendered my life and future to Him, I've had no option but to trust Him for everything. Has He been faithful to me? Again and again He has gone before me, opened doors and provided for my needs from His multiple resources. Only a good leader can be fully trusted. And God is a really good Leader!

---

[1] *Hymn "I Surrender All" is written by Judson W. VanDeventer, 1896.*

[2] *Jeremiah 17:5, 7 NIV*

[3] *Isaiah 30:21 NIV*

[4] *Waco, Texas—location of Baylor University*

Baylor University,
Waco Texas

5

Fulfillment Of A Dream

*The LORD'S unfailing love surrounds the man
who trusts in him.*

Psalms 32:10b NIV

The year I completed my Ph.D. at Baylor was the most rapidly changing year of my life. I finished with a 4.0 GPA and all my educational expenses were completely paid. Newspaper reporters came to my house for a feature article. T.V. cameras were at my graduation ceremony and featured me on the 10 o'clock evening news.

Job Search

With my doctoral degree in hand, I pressed forward to find employment as a New Testament professor in a college or seminary. I prayed and fasted for God's favor and guidance.

I sent out resumes to colleges and seminaries on both coasts and many places in between. At one point, an Oregon seminary offered me a position in Old Testament Studies. Because I was determined to find a job in New Testament Studies, I turned it down.

In April, I became one of two final candidates for a New Testament position at an Ohio seminary. The other finalist got the job; I got the regret letter. I was used to these letters. But this one was particularly discouraging, knowing I had almost gotten my dream job. It caused my heart to sink. A silent voice kept saying, *nobody is going to hire you as a quadriplegic.* In my disappointment, I committed it again to God and reminded Him of my need of a job.

The very next day I received a phone call from the academic dean at Mid-America Nazarene University[1] in Olathe, Kansas (a suburb of Kansas City). Though I had not applied there, the dean had heard about me completing the Ph.D. They needed a New Testament professor and offered me the job. After consulting the Lord, I called the dean back, accepted the position and signed a contract by mail.

Driving Challenge

With a contract in hand, I bought my first automobile, a new Dodge van. Texas Vocational Rehabilitation was willing to alter it for me to drive from my wheelchair. Because of my paralysis, I hadn't driven an automobile since I was 16.

My VR counselor arranged for a Baylor graduate student to help me practice driving again using hand controls in a Baylor Drivers-Ed car. After two weeks of driving practice, using my mostly paralyzed hands, I was ready to start driving my own new van.

In the meantime, my van was in San Antonio being customized for my needs. A wheelchair lift and power doors were installed so that I could come and go independently. Waiting was hard!

Yet the astounding changes occurring in my life in 1977 were happening at a fast pace. I signed a contract to teach in April, received my Ph.D. diploma in May, purchased my van in June, did two weeks Driver's Ed training in July, received my first power wheelchair through VR in July, and drove my customized van for the first time on August 1st from San Antonio to Waco (nearly 200 miles) at night.

The next day, August 2nd, I took my driver's test, parallel parked correctly, and received my Texas driver's license. On August 3rd a moving truck loaded our belongings and I drove my new van to Oklahoma City. The next day I completed the 600 miles to Olathe.

Housing Challenge

My first challenge upon arriving in Olathe was to find suitable housing. The university placed me (and my parents) in temporary student housing, with the understanding we had to be out the last week of August. I searched for a rental house, but found nothing workable for a wheelchair. I looked into buying a suitable house. Nothing!

In a desperate search, a realtor rode with me in my van on a visual search for a house without steps. We found a small house built on a cement slab; no steps whatsoever.

There wasn't a "for sale" sign in the yard. We rang the doorbell and asked the owner if he was interested in selling his house. The man gave the realtor a stare of unbelief. "As a matter of fact, I am."

We learned he had just gone through a divorce, his wife had moved out with the furniture and he was sleeping on the floor with a mattress. He had previously listed the house, but had pulled it because of no interest.

We made him an offer, he countered; we agreed and signed a contract. The house was ideal for a wheelchair and became my home for 21 years.

The next challenge was to obtain a loan quickly. Many loan applications were awaiting approval when mine arrived. The realtor said he would explain our unique circumstances and request quick approval, but he could promise nothing.

Amazingly my loan was made a priority and approved promptly, stunning even my realtor. We were able to move into our new house the same day students were moving into the university housing. As someone has said, "God has perfect timing; never early, never late. It takes a little patience and it takes a lot of faith. But it's worth the wait."

Fruit of God's Leadership

While others were moving my books into my new house, I rolled into my university classroom for the first time as a professor. The moment was surreal! Would the students respect me as a professor in a wheelchair?

They did in a big way! They made my first teaching year thoroughly enjoyable and successful. This was the culmination of many years of preparation, the fulfillment of a dream and the beginning of an exciting new chapter in my life.

In reflecting on God's leadership with me in 1977, it is plain to see He's a good leader. If I had gotten a teaching position in one of the colleges or seminaries where I had applied earlier, I never would have met Jane. My future hinged on fully trusting God and submitting to His wisdom, guidance and timing.

When Abraham's servant arrived in the city of Nahor, he went to the community well for water for his camels and men. At that very place and time he found Rebekah, a bride for Abraham's son, as Abraham had commissioned him to do.[2] What amazing timing! I didn't know it, but God was directing me to the right place at the right time to obtain a bride for myself. Truly God *"is faithful in all he does."*[3]

---

[1] *Mid-America Nazarene College in 1977*

[2] *Genesis 24:1-61*

[3] *Psalm 33:4b*

MidAmerica

6

First Glimpses

Many waters cannot quench love.

Song of Songs 8:7a

Jane was in her second year as a student at Mid-America when I arrived as a new professor. I was barely 36; she was 19. Jane's first glimpse of me was memorable. Her own testimony was she saw me come out of a classroom building in my power chair, speed across the campus mall and disappear into the Campus Center. Her eyes riveted on me with fascination. She said to herself, *I don't know if he is a new student, new professor, or a visitor, but I've got to meet him.*

The first time I remember meeting Jane was in the foyer of the big College Church on a Sunday morning. She walked up, somewhat timidly, "I'm Jane." Then she said with excitement, "I'm going to be in your Johannine Literature class next semester."

My reply was matter-of-fact, "That's nice. I'll enjoy having you as a student." I didn't have a clue who she was or anything about her.

When the new semester began, Jane was in my Johannine Literature class as promised, sitting on the front row with her Bible, notebook and pen in hand, ready to go. Before the course was completed, I knew she was a diligent and bright student. But frankly, I noticed little else.

Unscheduled Visit

A year later, one Sunday evening after church, unbeknown to me, Jane and her friend followed me home. I had gotten out of my van and was talking with my father in the driveway when Jane drove up in her parent's old Buick. She jumped out of the car and ran up the driveway to say hi and meet my father. My mother did the hospitable thing and invited the two girls in for tea.

This picture is actually amusing—a college co-ed following at a distance her single professor home after church to see where he lived and to meet his parents. She made it appear spontaneous.

I think Jane knew who my father was but had never met my mother. In our living room was a nice cuckoo clock from the Black Forest in Germany, a gift from my sister. During the evening, on the hour, the clock went off and out popped a cuckoo. In a flash, Jane was on her feet and ran to the clock to look at the action up close.

What was my mother's first impression of Jane? She thought Jane was full of energy and a bit high strung. I can still see Jane that evening—bouncy, chatty, lively, and vivacious.

I had planned to do work in my study/library that evening. Silently I hoped Jane and her friend would leave soon so I could prepare for my Monday classes. It didn't happen.

Jane's unscheduled visit occurred before she worked in my department as an assistant. Any way you look at it, her behavior that night was daring. And bit annoying for a busy professor!

College Senior

Jane's last two courses with me before graduation were actually her two favorite college courses: Hermeneutics I & II. She thoroughly loved these classes because they further equipped her with the principles and tools necessary for studying the Bible more deeply on her own.

Hermeneutics II applied the principles learned in Hermeneutics I. Students were each assigned a passage in Ephesians to carefully exegete. I required them to provide a written copy of their exegesis for other students to follow during the oral class presentations. A sermon outline, based on the exegesis, was included.

Jane chose Ephesians 2:11-22 and did a superb job. In fact hers was so good, I used her exegesis as a prototype for other students thereafter.

Jane served as an assistant for professors in the department of Biblical and Theological Studies during her senior year. It was a paid position of distinct honor. As a quad, I needed her help more than other professors, and we began to develop a more personal friendship.

During finals week her last semester, Jane had her own exams plus student papers to grade for me. She was behind on grading a difficult assignment for my very large New Testament Survey class. Consequently, papers weren't graded when I needed them to calculate final grades.

In the meantime, Jane's Greek class was going to a Greek restaurant as their finale of the year. She missed her class outing to grade my papers and told me frankly, "You owe me a dinner out." At this point, she knew the strength of her love for me, but I was still unaware.

7

Answer At The Door

Many are the plans in the mind of a man, but it is the purpose of the Lord that will stand.

Proverbs 19:21 ESV

A momentous series of events unfolded during May of Jane's graduation year. It was like a May drama and I was pulled into it, having never volunteered for the part.

Christyne

The drama began early in May on a Sunday in Falls City, Nebraska. I was a guest speaker at a Nazarene church. A student from that church, Christyne, rode back with me to Kansas City after the evening service. During our conversation she said, "Prof, may I ask you a question?"

"Sure."

"Have you ever thought about getting married?"

I admired her courage but thought to myself, *Students these days are getting bold.*

I gave her an honest answer: "Yes, but I've decided against it. As a quadriplegic, it would be too difficult for a wife."

"I don't think you should feel that way. I think if the right person came along, it could work."

I was impressed with her confidence but thought, "she doesn't understand the extent of my paralysis." Our conversation then went on to other subjects.

Randy

Shortly after the May commencement, Randy, one of my graduating seniors, was preparing to take his first pastorate and was painting the exterior of my house in the interval.

On a warm day the latter part of May, I took him a glass of water outdoors. He sat down on the grass to talk with me during the break.

He spoke unexpectedly, "Prof, have you ever thought about getting married?" I thought to myself, *This question sounds strangely familiar.*

I replied as I had a few weeks before, "Yes, but I've decided against it as long as I'm in a wheelchair."

He responded, "Maybe you shouldn't think that way. In fact I know someone who is interested in dating you."

I was startled! "You do? Who?"

With a big smile on his face, he said, "Jane Peterson."

"How do you know this?"

His reply was, "She told me."

The Secret

I later learned that Randy had talked several times to Jane before graduation. He would say, "We've got to find you a husband before you leave the campus. Whom are you interested in on the campus?" Jane would always reply: "Nobody."

Randy, however, would not be deterred. He would come into the office repeatedly with the same question. Finally Jane hedged a bit, "There's no student on this campus I'm interested in."

Randy replied, "Surely there's someone."

Eventually, Jane's resolve weakened and she revealed her secret, "Ok. There's someone I like, but he's not a student. If I tell you, you've got to promise you won't tell anyone."

Predictably he replied, "Of course, I won't tell anyone."

Jane let the cat out of the bag. "I like Dr. Adams."

Randy erupted with excitement. "That's wonderful! I'll tell him."

Jane was horrified. "Randy, you promised you wouldn't tell!"

Randy grinned. "That's so wonderful."

While painting my house, Randy, in his excitement, let the same cat out of the bag.

But of course it didn't end there.

Dr. Larry Fine

When Jane learned Randy had told me her secret, she turned red. Bewildered what to do next, Jane went to one of my colleagues, entered his office, and closed the door.

"Dr. Fine, I've got a problem."

"Take a seat and tell me what the problem is."

She relayed the story and confessed, "I don't know what to do. I'm embarrassed to ever see Dr. Adams again." She felt like a little schoolgirl on the playground soon to be relentlessly teased: "I know who you like."

My colleague looked at Jane, and asked her directly, "Do you love him?"

"Yes!"

"Do you think you could handle being married to him?"

"Yes, I think so."

Jane at 22

Dr. Fine was my close friend. Our friendship went back to our college and seminary years, and had grown greatly during our teaching years together in the same department. Dr. Fine said to Jane, "Don't worry about a thing; I'll take care of this."

Jane panicked. She wondered, *What have I just done?*

When Jane left, Dr. Fine immediately walked down the hall to my office, entered, and closed the door. "Let's go for a coffee break."

I agreed and we drove to a hangout for student and faculty not far from campus. At the restaurant table, he began, "Wes, have you thought recently about getting married?"

Three times now in May I had heard these familiar words. I felt a conspiracy unfolding. I pounded the table, "What is going on?"

My colleague began talking very frankly about Jane's respect and affection for me.

"I think she would be interested in marriage. You need to give this some prayerful thought and consideration, or you need to put distance between you and her."

Years of thinking marriage for me would never work caused me to respond negatively. "Then I'll put distance between us."

Dr. Fine requested, "Will you at least pray about it?"

I was on the horns of a dilemma. Believing strongly in the power of prayer, I couldn't say, "No, I won't pray about it." I agreed, but I was hedging. "I'm 99.9% sure the answer is no."

Internal Wrestling

I was an athlete before paralysis, lettering in baseball and basketball. My accident instantly reduced me to an embarrassing state of physical incapacity.

All four of my extremities are affected by paralysis. Although I can move my arms, I cannot voluntarily move my fingers or thumbs. I have not moved a toe or leg voluntarily in over 50 years.

Quadriplegics go through extensive physical, spiritual, emotional and social upheaval, followed by major adjustments for the quad and his family. Quadriplegics' capabilities are so limited, when compared to their previous functioning, they tend to see mostly what they cannot do. Only gradually do they learn how to use what is left, and some never adjust.

Initially the idea of my ever driving an automobile as a quad seemed preposterous, even scary. Not until 19 years after my paralysis did I have that breakthrough and began to drive again. Since then I've safely driven three vans from my wheelchair with hand controls over 350,000 miles. I've completely worn out two converted vans; presently I have over 110,000 miles on my third van.

The prospect of driving was daunting to me for many years, and being married as a quad seemed preposterous as well. The impossibility loomed larger than an immovable mountain! The Lord had to work on this stronghold in my mind.

Proverbs 3:5-6

God helped me over the years to conquer many fears and impossible goals.

These two verses were God's deposit of faith in me for my impossible journey. Whenever I have faced an important life decision, the Lord has always brought me back to His instructive promise in Scripture—

> *Don't lean on your own limited understanding;*
> *trust Me and let Me direct your path.*[1]

Through the years these words of Scripture enabled me to find a posture of faith, trust and confidence in God for my struggles.

What I was now facing was certainly an important life decision that would hugely influence my future destiny.

Everybody's three most important decisions of life are:

❖ The choice of a Master
❖ The choice of a Mission
❖ The choice of a Mate

I felt keenly the weight of my decision and the direction it would take me. I had to know from God what He thought about this. I was so earnest, I determined to fast three days in order to press into God with prayer. During the fast, I was surprised how clearly God spoke to me and equally surprised at what He said!

Providential Tension

As I was praying about Jane, my parents were in their mid 70's. They had been my faithful, loving, and diligent caregivers for 22 years. They had remained focused and dedicated to assist me in fulfilling my calling. Their excellent care for my needs as a quadriplegic, including dressing and getting me out bed every morning, had enabled me to function and remain in good health while earning four university and seminary degrees.

For years I had prayed about what to do when my parents were no longer able to physically care for me. As I was praying and fasting about Jane, my mindset about not marrying began to weaken as God spoke affirmatively about Jane as a good marriage partner. The internal voice of God spoke clearer and clearer during my three day fast.

My fast came to a grand finale on the third day at a Sunday morning service. The pastor was preaching from Acts 12 about Herod imprisoning Peter and James. After killing James, Herod intended to do the same with Peter. But in the night, an angel of the Lord came to Peter's cell and supernaturally delivered him. Peter walked to the house where he knew the church would be in an all-night prayer meeting for his deliverance.

The correlation here between prayer by the church and Peter's supernatural deliverance is clear! Prayer changes things! When Peter knocked at the house, Rhoda, the maid, was so startled she left Peter standing outside the locked door. In her excitement, she rushed into the prayer meeting with the happy news.[2]

The pastor, after a pause in his morning message, gave the punch line: "For some of you, your answer is knocking at the door."

The Holy Spirit spoke these words emphatically to my heart, and I wept at God's goodness. I was now confident that the startling new development with Jane was His doing.

---

[1] My paraphrase of Proverbs 3:5-6

[2] Acts 12:1-19

Jane On The Arm Of Her Father

8

Courtship & Covenant

Houses and wealth are inherited from parents,
but a prudent wife is from the LORD.

Proverbs 19:14 NIV

My father worked as a steak chef at one of Kansas City's nicest restaurants. As an honored employee, he had four complimentary dinner tickets. I owed Jane a dinner out since she missed her Greek finale because of me. I fulfilled my obligation by taking her on a double date with my parents.

This was the perfect opportunity to get our courtship started. Jane later told me, "The double date made it much less stressful than going with you the first time by myself."

Courting

There is a big difference between courting and dating. Dating is spending time with the opposite sex without commitment to the future. Courting is intentional time spent with the opposite sex that is unto marriage and covenant. Courting is the time when love can begin to awaken and develop between both individuals as God intends.

Dating usually involves multiple relationships; courting is monogamous, like betrothal in biblical times. I was not interested in experimental dating in order to find a suitable match, an approach that leads to temptation and oftentimes heartache.

Courting is done with both God and marriage in view. I was confident that God had spoken clearly to me about Jane, but I didn't use that as leverage. I waited until after our formal engagement seven months later to tell her, making sure in the meantime our motives were right.

A week or so after our dinner together with my parents, I invited Jane to a Kansas City Royals vs. New York Yankees baseball game at the end of May. It was our first time together alone and proved to be interesting.

Journey Begins

I grew up during the golden age of major league baseball. Radio carried daily a "game of the day" broadcast. Though I lived in Oklahoma, my favorite baseball team was the Brooklyn Dodgers. These were the Dodgers' "glory days" when Don Newcombe, Johnny Podres, Jackie Robinson, Gill Hodges, Duke Snyder, Roy Campanella, and Pee Wee Reese played at Ebbet's Field. I had many fond memories of baseball.

Jane, however, knew very little about the game. I endeavored to teach her that night. To my dismay, she thought the game was dumb and boring. That's a real shock to a lifetime baseball fan who lettered in the sport!

I was patient and taught her one rule after another during the game. Time and again she argued with me as if I were the inventor of baseball and its rules. I don't remember the final score of the ballgame, but I will forever remember the outcome of my introduction to Jane on a social level. As a footnote, Jane came to enjoy baseball and loved to attend at least one Royals' game every summer. What a great convert!

Seeking Confirmation

During the summer of 1980, Jane and I fell in love. Maybe I should say I fell in love with Jane, because arguably she had already fallen for me. The more I got to know her, the more I appreciated the unique woman she was. When God said, *"it is not good for the man to be alone,"* He added—*"I will make a helper suitable for him."*[1] Little did I know initially what a suitable, even perfect, helpmate God was giving me.

My parents loved Jane from the beginning. My sister, Eileen, who was living on the east coast, came for a summer visit with her children in their camper. I valued greatly my sister's discernment, believing it would be invaluable. Almost from the moment Eileen met Jane, my sister liked her and believed she would be a great wife for me. My two nephews and niece also loved her. Obviously Jane was passing the "tests" with my family.

Everyone at the college who knew us was excited about our interest in one another. I even inquired of the academic dean who had hired me, and he thought Jane and I were a great match.

Jane's parents, however, were not so sure. Understandably, they were concerned about our age difference, 16 years, and about me being a quadriplegic. Typically, spinal-cord-injury quadriplegics do not live long and their health declines as the years pass. The average life span of a quadriplegic after injury is 16 to 17 years. I had already been paralyzed for 23 years but was still in excellent health.

I now realize what a miracle of preservation I am. Six weeks after my injury, my main doctor told my parents, "I'm sorry to tell you this, but your son will not live long and will not be in good health while he lives."

As I write these words, I'm in my 55th year as a quad confined to a wheelchair. Moreover, I've not been a patient in a hospital for 53 years. This is a preservation miracle!

Fifteen months after my accident, God awakened me in the night and told me He planned to heal me. I believed Him then and I believe Him now! If God is bold enough to promise a quadriplegic healing, I'm bold enough to believe Him! This I know is my story: God has been faithful and sustained me physically in a most amazing way.

Jane's primary care physician told her a few years ago that she should enter me into the Guinness Book of World Records. He said, "I cannot imagine any quadriplegic living 50 years in their condition." But with God, anything is possible!

Jane's parents were conservative in every way. They believed, and justifiably so, that their daughter was somehow destined for greatness. They could not see how she could achieve greatness by marrying a quadriplegic. I was sympathetic with their concerns. Nevertheless, I forthrightly asked them permission to "court" their daughter. They said yes, but hoped no doubt that it would come to nothing.

The Big Test

As the months passed, our love grew until it was evident that we both were totally serious about marriage. I talked to her extensively about my physical limitations and care-giving needs. She was always undaunted!

After six months, I told Jane that our relationship needed to be tested in another way. Before we made decisions about engagement and marriage, she needed to participate with my parents in taking physical care of me. Only then would we really know her aptitude and interest in being married to a quadriplegic.

After watching my parents assist me as caregivers, Jane took on sole responsibility for my care for one week. She faced every issue a caregiver would face in taking care of me morning, noon and night for seven days. Again she was undaunted by the challenge or the tasks. In fact, after one week, she was ecstatic that she had passed the test!

Then her parents had to face their worst fears. I asked Jane's father for permission to marry his daughter. He tried evading the question by saying that Jane was old enough to make the decision herself.

I said, "Clyde, that is not God's way. The father and mother have responsibility from God for a son or daughter until they are grown and married."

I told him that he and Marcile must participate in this decision—"yes" or "no." I had not anticipated this hurdle and thought to myself, *This is more difficult than it needs to be.*

I asked Jane's father again directly, "May I marry your daughter." Finally, he said yes. Once he said yes, both Clyde and Marcile received me completely and became the best father-in-law and mother-in-law a man could have. I came to love them dearly, as they did me.

Engagement

In December, before Christmas, I took Jane to a nice restaurant in Kansas City where I asked her to marry me. She responded with an unhesitating YES!

In the denomination where I was ordained, most ministers' wives had a wedding ring but not an engagement ring. Therefore, I gave Jane an expensive Seiko watch as my engagement gift, which her mother helped me select.

Jane and I tentatively planned our wedding to be the last of May 1981, after I had finished all final exams and submitted all final grades to the Registrar's office.

Several important people to us wanted us to be married earlier than May. My sister and brother-in-law, who was a career officer in the Air Force, were going back to Germany in February with their family to live there for three more years. Eileen begged me to get married in January.

Jane and I, however, felt we needed the time until May to continue growing together and for making all the necessary plans for the wedding and our future.

Our courting year was especially busy for Jane. She was teaching First Year Greek at her Alma Mater and taking courses on a M.A. degree in Classics at Kansas University. There was no time for a wedding and honeymoon until May when classes ended for us both. Thus we continued courting through the winter and spring months, finally selecting May 29th as the big day. This was almost one year to the day after our first baseball game date.

Wedding

Ezekiel described his wife as *"the delight of my eyes."*[2] During our courtship, my love for Jane grew immensely. She was the delight of my eyes on our wedding day.

Jane and I were married at College Church on MidAmerica campus on May 29, 1981. Our marriage was unusual for multiple reasons! I, a college professor, was marrying my most illustrious former student. Our difference in age, over 16 years, was also unusual. I was 39 and Jane was barely 23, having had a birthday only two weeks before. But most startling of all, I was a quadriplegic and confined to a wheelchair for 23 years, only two days less than my bride's age.

Jane wore the wedding dress her mother had worn 31 years before. It was a full-length satin dress, with a long train, and lace trim. She was a most beautiful bride as she came down the aisle on the arm of her proud father.

Several hundred wedding guests gathered to witness our wedding vows. Among the guests were many extended family members of the bride and the groom, close friends, students, and faculty.

It was a joyous occasion! We exchanged wedding rings at the church altar, acknowledging their covenant significance. Jane selected a passage from the book of Ruth to be sung as her marriage testimony:

> *Entreat me not to leave thee, or to return from following after thee: for whither thou goest, I will go; and where thou lodgest, I will lodge: thy people shall be my people, and thy God my God.*[3]

Marriage Covenant

Jane and I both had a rich heritage of marriage faithfulness modeled for us as we came to the marriage altar. Jane's paternal and maternal grandparents both celebrated 50 years of marriage; her parents celebrated 57 years of marriage before her father died. Likewise, my paternal and maternal grandparents both celebrated more than 50 years of marriage; my parents celebrated 58 years.

We understood clearly and agreed emphatically that our marriage vows were covenant vows, made before God and many witnesses, and must never be broken.

Marriage is a covenant![4] It is the very first covenant God made with the human race.[5] Covenant is God's way of establishing a permanent relationship between one man and one woman with enduring purpose.

God is a covenant God! God's love is "covenant love"; God's grace is "covenant grace"; God's promises are "covenant promises"; God's redemption is "covenant redemption"; and marriage for a covenant believer is a "covenant marriage."

Covenant means marriage is a lifetime commitment that must never be broken. Marriage is a covenant to love, cherish and be faithful to one's spouse for life. Love is a commitment, not just an emotion.

Covenant Instruction

In Christ, marriage partners are equal heirs of God's gracious gift of life. One is not greater and the other lesser. One is not more important before God than the other.

But we knew our roles as marriage partners were described differently in Ephesians 5:22-33. We understood that I was to love my bride as Christ loves the Church—a sacrificing and sanctifying love that brings out the beauty of the Bride. We also understood that the Church's submission to Christ represents the wife's submission to her husband, involving being loyal, faithful, devoted, pure and loving.

Jane and I believed strongly that Ephesians 5:22-33 encapsulated God's wisdom for living out our marriage covenant. With this conviction, we said our vows to one another—

I take you to be my lawfully
wedded wife/husband,
to have and to hold
from this day forward,
for better or for worse,
for richer or for poorer,
in sickness and in health,
to love and to cherish
till death do us part
according to God's holy commandment
and thereto I pledge you my love.

As we turned around for our exit, I marked Jane as exclusively mine by leaving my wheelchair tire mark on her beautiful satin train.

---

[1] *Genesis 2:18-25*

[2] *Ezekiel 24:16*

[3] *Ruth 1:16 KJV*

[4] *Malachi 2:14 NIV*

[5] *Genesis 2:18-25*

9

Early Days

Let him kiss me with the kisses of his mouth—
For your love is better than wine.

Song of Songs 1:2 NKJV

There is not a more wholesome romantic scene than when the bride and bridegroom depart for their first night together and thereby embark on a lifetime journey.

I saved as much money as I could from my meager salary for our honeymoon. It was by no means a big stash! It was not nearly enough to fly somewhere nice for a week or two, so I decided to make it a significant honeymoon as well as fun on a smaller budget.

Honeymoon

After staying our first night in Ottawa (Kansas, not Canada), we drove to Oklahoma City and the suburb of Bethany where I had lived for six years, finished high school and completed two college degrees.

Jane's mother had attended the same college, so Jane and I had some common history there. Jane enjoyed seeing where I lived with my parents across the street from the high school and near the college campus.

On Sunday I gave Jane a guided tour of the campus. That evening we attended a service at the big College Church. To our surprise, we encountered Jane's Uncle Kenny and Aunt Deloris, who lived in Oklahoma City.

The next day we drove 20 miles west to El Reno, where I was living when I was paralyzed. We visited El Reno High School, the church I attended as a teenager, and the little hamburger diners near the high school, where I ate most school days. I still like to go to El Reno and get one of those hamburgers. They taste better there than anywhere else in the world, testifying to the powerful association of nostalgia and one's taste buds.

I showed Jane the high school gym where I lettered in basketball my sophomore year. For Jane to see the landmarks of my youth, both before and immediately after I was paralyzed, was a special participation in my personal history. She loved hearing my stories while visiting these sights. This may seem like a strange honeymoon, but we were both enjoying it and one another.

Miscommunication

All marriages have their moments of classic miscommunication. Our first one came on our honeymoon. I drove my van while sitting in my power wheelchair. I am 6' 1" and sit fairly high in the chair. The floor of the van had to be lowered in order to give me adequate windshield visibility. Traffic lights in those days were suspended in the air over the center of the intersection and I had to bend way over to see them.

I decided to use my bride to alert me about traffic signals when they changed. We were sitting at a red traffic light and I told Jane to let me know when it turned green. Then I added, "Okay?"

She replied, "Okay!" At that I bolted through the intersection.

She screamed! "What are you doing? It's still red!"

"You said 'Okay.'"

Still shocked, she burst out, "I said, 'Okay' I will tell you when it changed."

Fortunately, no cars were coming and there were no policemen in the vicinity, and no harm was done. We had many good laughs about that afterwards, but not at the time.

Eccentric Interest

After Oklahoma, our honeymoon continued to Dallas. I introduced Jane to one of my eccentric interests when traveling—i.e., visiting noteworthy universities and seminaries.

We visited the famous First Baptist Church in downtown Dallas that had only two pastors in 85 years. George W. Truett pastored it 45 years; his successor, W.A. Criswell, pastored the church 40 years. Both Southern Baptist preachers were renowned as great expositors of the Word.

While at Baylor, I visited Dallas First Baptist one Sunday just to hear Dr. Criswell expound the Scriptures. I was not disappointed! His brilliant message on Stephen in Acts 7 impacted me both as a preacher and teacher of the Word.

I also showed Jane Dallas Theological Seminary, Southern Methodist University, Southwest Baptist Theological Seminary, and Texas Christian University. Jane was slow to gain appreciation for all these campus visits. But after a while she came to enjoy visiting college campuses as much as I did—literally!

Next stop was Waco, and Baylor University. I introduced her to some of my former professors, and showed her my doctoral dissertation on the shelf in Moody Library. Jane saw rooms where I had Ph.D. seminars and presented papers.

Jane especially enjoyed the Baylor visit and all the stories I told her about my years there. She was growing in her knowledge of the man she loved and had married a week before.

On Sunday I proudly introduced my bride to the congregation where my parents and I attended during my Baylor years. The precious people at the First Nazarene Church greatly enjoyed meeting Jane. We spent five days in Waco.

A year or so later, I was invited to be senior pastor of that congregation, an invitation that I declined even though I would have enjoyed being with my many friends there and being near Baylor again. But God's purpose and direction for Jane and I was different.

Southbound

South of Waco we visited the University of Texas at Austin—the biggest university in America at that time. Two sights at U.T. especially interested me—their famous football stadium and the Lyndon B. Johnson Presidential Library and Museum.

After Austin we drove south to San Antonio. Jane and I have visited many famous cities in the world—New York City, Washington D.C., San Francisco, Seattle, London, Paris, Strassborg, Brussels, beautiful cities in

Switzerland, Rio de Janeiro and Sao Paulo in Brazil. It seems to surprise people when I tell them that one of our favorite cities is San Antonio, Texas.

Our 25th Wedding Anniversary revisit to San Antonio was one of the most enjoyable five days we ever spent together.

San Antonio's River Walk is as quaint and romantic a place as any sight we have ever visited in the world.[1]

Honeymoon in San Antonio

After San Antonio, Jane put her feet in the Gulf of Mexico at Galveston. We visited the mammoth Astrodome at Houston, America's first indoor baseball and football stadium.

Three Weeks

Before returning to our home in Olathe, we also visited Louisiana, Arkansas, and Missouri. We were gone a total of three weeks, visited five states, and ate at what seemed like a hundred Red Lobsters.

Our pattern was to eat a late breakfast somewhere like Denny's, then eat a late lunch 3:30-4:00 at a Red Lobster—dinner size meals for less than four dollars at the time. Typically, in the evening, we would eat something light like pizza. This was our method of making our little money go a long way on a three-week honeymoon, and we had a blast!

Adjustments

When Jane and I returned home, we had the rest of the summer to adjust to living together. I was working on a theological writing assignment and preaching on some weekends. Jane was working at the college library and taking a summer class at KU.

In the fall, our lives were busy again with academia. I taught a full schedule of college classes, led the Friday night prayer meetings, and taught a small Bible study on Acts. Jane continued working in the college library part-time and taking courses on her M.A. degree such as Classical Greek, Latin, German classes and a course in Greek Mythology.

A big adjustment for Jane, our first year, was living in the same house with my parents. At times it was stressful for her; at other times it was a big blessing. Before marriage, Jane had little experience in the kitchen. My mother was the best mentor a new bride could have and Jane learned well. She came to surpass my mother as a marvelous cook.

Jane with Wes' Parents In Olathe Kitchen

After our first year, my father wisely chose to move and let Jane and me have the house alone. This was no ordinary move for my parents. They were 76 and 77 when Dad became pastor of a small church in

Brownwood, Texas.

It was nice having our little 1200 square foot home to ourselves. Yet it did put an extra workload on Jane, since there was no longer shared labor. It also put greater financial pressure on us, since my parents had contributed to the utility bills.

Because of these changes, Jane chose to discontinue her M.A. studies. The pressures became considerably less and she never regretted her decision.

She had other adjustments—like being a professor's wife and going to faculty events. Though she was the youngest faculty spouse, Jane quickly became comfortable in her new role.

It was pure joy to have her by my side on Sundays when we went to church or on weekends when we ate out. We learned to pray together, play together, and do life together. We were seldom apart and enjoyed one another's company immensely. I had never been this happy, living life with my covenant bride, *"the delight of my eyes."*[2]

---

[1] *San Antonio has one of the largest Sea Worlds and a phenomenal botanical garden. And of course, there is the Alamo and numerous other interesting sights.*

[2] *Ezekiel 24:16*

10

A Holy Standard

Before you were born, I set you apart.

Jeremiah 1:5

Holiness is one of God's most defining characteristics. He is perfectly pure and sin cannot exist in His presence. Because God is holy, we too are called to be holy[1] by being set apart from all that is unholy.

To be set apart *by* God and *for* God is the high calling of every authentic believer. Some individuals are even set apart by God from birth for His own glory and sovereign purpose.[2]

Set Apart For His Glory[3]

At an early age Jane was set apart by God and for God. Her testimony about her high school years was like that of Jeremiah:

When Your words came, I ate them;
they were my joy and my heart's delight,
for I bear Your name, O LORD God Almighty.
I never sat in the company of revelers [partiers],
never made merry with them;
I sat alone because Your hand was on me.[4]

Jane distinguished herself academically in high school. Although she had friends, in many respects she was alone. She was serious minded and philosophical from a young age. She was more like a young scholar or mystic than a homecoming queen. Like Jeremiah, she sat alone[5] because God's hand was on her. The following three biblical values strengthened Jane in her being set apart for God in high school and afterwards.

Authority of Scripture

Jane believed strongly that the Bible was God's Word to us. She believed it was supernaturally inspired by the Holy Spirit and written through chosen human vessels. She believed the end-result is a Bible without error. She steadfastly believed that God's Word is pure (i.e., without humanistic mixture) and, like God himself, is fully trustworthy[6], timeless[7] and eternally relevant.[8]

In our subjective post-modern age, the objective standard of God's written Word must be recovered. As believers, we must know what we believe and why we believe it, based on the trustworthy authority of Scripture as our plumbline for life.

Secular humanism in our culture views moral absolutes as "outdated" and moral relativism is "in." Moral and spiritual relativism is hammered constantly through media, education, entertainment and socio-political correctness. This pervasive message is eroding the spiritual and moral foundations of marriage, the family, the church and the nation.

A survey found that 80% of evangelical unmarried young adults (18-29) are having sex before marriage.[9] Unless the Bible remains our plumbline of truth and morality, cultural relativism will become the norm in the church.

Where is the standard of God's Word as the bedrock truth? Jesus prayed for His disciples, *"Sanctify them by Your truth. Your word is truth."*[10] Jane was sanctified by the truth of God's Word. Her deep love for God and His written Word set her apart from the common lot.

Sanctification

Biblical sanctification means being set apart *from* what is impure and unholy, in order to be set apart *for* God who is pure and holy! How are we to be holy unto the Lord?[11] Jane believed the cross was powerful enough to make her pure and keep her pure in a sinful world.[12]

Jesus said, *"If you love me, keep My commandments."*[13] Jane loved Jesus and therefore obeyed Him. She committed herself to be sober-minded and to *"be holy"*[14] as the grace of God makes possible. She sought to walk before God in holiness, the fear of the Lord, faith and sincere obedience.

The fragrance of her life had a sanctifying effect on all those around her, myself included. Loving Jesus with abandonment empowered her to keep herself pure and undefiled by the world, while impacting others. She kept her *"heart with all diligence."*[15]

In high school, Jane's classmates were experimenting with alcohol and sex. She was horrified on Mondays when the girls glibly talked about their weekends with guys. In the midst of her peers' lifestyle, Jane continued to embrace God and His standard of purity.

Jane understood that sexual sin is wrong—not because sex is wrong but because, outside the marriage bond and covenant, it violates God's moral law and spiritually defiles those involved.

Jane was sensitive in her spirit to anything spiritually unclean. She was extremely cautious about what she let her eyes see or ears hear. When she saw sinful things with her photographic mind, she found it difficult to get the image out of her mind. She resolved, *"I will set nothing wicked ["no vile thing," NIV] before my eyes. . .it shall not cling to me."*[16] Like the Psalmist, she would *"turn [her] eyes away from worthless things."*[17]

Jane seldom watched T.V. for this reason and almost never went to movies. She would ponder, *what does God think about T.V., entertainment or the movie?* She often said, "Whatever we are entertained by and laugh at, we will find much easier to compromise with. If we do not hate evil, we will tend to compromise with it all day long."

Her heart was repulsed by anything vulgar, immoral, violent, coarse, anti-God, or contrary to a biblical worldview. When her friends wanted to watch a video or go see a movie as entertainment, she usually declined. She refused to be entertained by darkness lest, as Jesus said, her light become darkness. In a measure true of few people, Jane was resolute not to compromise at any time or in any place.

The Bible testifies Jesus was anointed above all others. Why? Not because He was deity; rather, *"because He loved righteousness and hated wickedness."*[18] We are chosen to become like Him!

Jesus modeled the core principle that we cannot fully love God if we do not love what He loves and hate what He hates. Sometimes we do one or the other of these strong responses, but seldom do we exercise both of them intentionally at once. Jesus did! So did Jane!

Spiritual Intimacy

Loving God goes hand in hand with pleasing God. Pleasing God should be part of our love language with Him. Jane's goal was to please God with the way she lived her life. Like Paul, she wished to *"please Him in every way"*[19]—because of love. She believed that love and the desire to please the Beloved were both possible by the grace of God and the power of the Holy Spirit.

Scripture distinguishes between living to please men and living to please God. Many Christians, perhaps most, live to please men more than they live to please God. Paul resolved, *"We speak not as pleasing men, but [pleasing] God who tests our hearts."*[20]

Jane's motivation to please God and experience His approval was primary for her, not secondary as with many sincere believers. She pursued God relentlessly in intimacy out of a pure heart.

On two different occasions Jane did 40-day water and juice fasts, while seeking God's face. In some seasons she would be caught up in God's Word and read it day and night for hours. At times Jane would get up in the middle of the night and go to the living room to meet with God—because of love.

God says concerning a special category of people who choose what pleases Him and hold fast to His

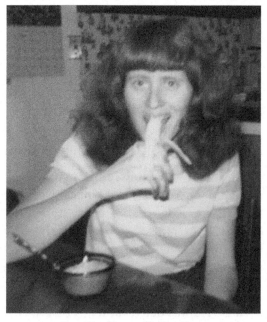

Jane Breaking a 40-Day Fast

covenant, *"better than sons and daughters; I will give them an everlasting name that will not be cut off."*[21] Jane faithfully chose what pleased God and tenaciously held fast to God's covenant of love as one truly set apart for Him.

One manifestation of God's glory is when God's people, through spiritual intimacy, are transformed into the likeness of the Lord Jesus. The foremost reason God works *"in all things"*[22] for our good is to conform us *"to the likeness of His Son."*[23]

Paul calls the glory of becoming like Jesus Christ the *"surpassing glory"* and a glory that lasts, not fades.[24] How do we participate in the surpassing glory of being like the Lord Jesus? We do so by gazing on His beauty and beholding His face in the intimacy of worship and prayer, and by engaging with Him through His Word and meditation.

We experience the radiance of His glory the nearer we get to Him and the longer we stay in His presence. During her last five years, Jane stayed longer in His presence. She became more quiet and confident, spoke less but with more impact and authority. To an amazing extent, she was set apart by God for God's glory. She was truly one of God's favorites and clearly reflected His image.

Set Apart For His Purpose[25]

God chose Jane for a specific purpose. She knew that from a young age, though the specifics she didn't grasp till much later. To be chosen and set apart for God's glory and purpose is an election for service, to bring blessing to others. It's God's sovereign right to choose certain people to accomplish specific redemptive purposes without explaining His choices.

God is governed, in all His choices, always by His wisdom, love, mercy and moral integrity. Jane, similar to Jacob and his descendants, was chosen for a specific purpose of God that would become clear later.

When Jane enrolled in college, she chose a Music major. At the beginning of her sophomore year, she changed to Biblical Studies. Why?

During the summer before her second year of college, Jane accompanied her grandmother to a regional church gathering where she heard a missionary speak from South Korea. The Holy Spirit greatly impacted her heart during the message.

She had been asking God for understanding about His specific purpose for her life. She was moved in her heart to offer her life to the Lord for ministry, telling God she was willing to serve Him on the mission field.

For some time there had been in Jane a gnawing desire to study God's Word more deeply as life's most important book and a treasure that would last forever. God was saying yes to this deep desire within her.

To nobody's surprise Jane excelled in Greek and in Biblical Studies. Soon it became apparent that she had an extraordinary aptitude for languages. Over the years she studied Greek, Hebrew, Latin, German, French, Spanish, and Portuguese.

During her senior year in college, the Department of Religion had comprehensive exams for majors covering Old Testament, New Testament, Systematic Theology, Historical Theology, Ethics, etc. Her scores on these exams were the highest ever made at that college. As far as I know, her scores never were surpassed. Eventually the exams, because of their difficulty, were completely dropped.

Set Apart To Be A Bride

We are all created for love and for God's glory. When we encounter and respond to Jesus' redeeming love, we are then set apart to become part of the collective Bride of Jesus Christ. Our wedding date is scheduled for the end of the age. Our Father sovereignly determines the day.

Jane and I often pondered the "coincidence" of her birth on Thursday, May 15, 1958 and my paralysis from the car wreck on Saturday, May 17, 1958—just two days apart. It was not clear I would live until mid to late Sunday afternoon.

In the same time frame, Jane's parents were undecided what to name their surprise daughter, having expected a boy. She was not named Jane until the same Sunday afternoon when it became evident I would live.

Jane and I often pondered this "coincidence" and wondered if perhaps this was no coincidence at all. In the end, Jane and I concluded that she— her name means "God's gracious gift"— was named Jane after my mother's intercession for me prevailed. Only then was it clear I was going to live and would need a gracious gift from God like Jane in my future.

Clearly, some things are appointed by God far in advance of their coming to pass.[26] Jane and I have never expected others to believe that our marriage was a divine set-up going back to May 18, 1958. But that's what we came to believe. When you've read the whole story, you can reach your own conclusion.

As a young girl, Jane would sometimes lie on her bed and pretend she was paralyzed. While lying motionless, she would try to imagine what it would be like to be unable to move. Who has ever heard of a little girl thinking such thoughts?

Was God starting to prepare Jane to be His gracious gift to a paralyzed man who would later be her favorite college professor? The "rest of the story"[27] will help you understand why we think the heavenly Father arranged our marriage.

---

[1] *1 Peter 1:13-16*

[2] *Jeremiah 1:5; Rom. 1:1*

[3] *Being set apart for God's glory and purpose means (1) being separated from sin and the spirit of the age, and (2) being set apart for Jesus Christ as a disciple who loves Him and keeps His commandments.*

[4] *Jeremiah 15:16-17 NIV*

[5] *Jeremiah 15:17*

[6] *Psalm 119:138, 140*

[7] *Psalm 119:144*

[8] *Psalm 119:89*

[9] *Relevant magazine, editor Cameron Strang (first issue March/April 2003), is a bimonthly magazine providing content on "God, life, and progressive culture".*

[10] *John 17:17*

[11] *1 Thessalonians 4:3-4*

[12] *Titus 2:11-12; 1 Pet. 1:13-16*

[13] *John 14:15 NKJV*

[14] *1 Peter 1:15,16*

[15] *Proverbs 4:23*

[16] *Psalm 101:3 NKJV*

[17] *Psalm 119:37 NLT*

[18] *Psalm 45:7; Hebrews 1:9*

[19] *cf. Colossians 1:10 NIV*

[20] *1 Thessalonians 2:4 NKJV*

[21] *Isaiah 56:4-5 NASB*

[22] *Romans 8:28 NIV*

[23] *Romans 8:29 NIV*

[24] *2 Corinthians 3:7-11 NIV*

[25] *Biblical "election" has to do with being set apart by God for a specific purpose that God chooses. In Romans 9 Paul uses the story of the twin sons of Isaac and Rebecca—Esau and Jacob—to explain "election." Before the twins were born or had done anything good or evil, God "chose" Jacob for a specific purpose. For what purpose did God choose Jacob? He chose Jacob, though Esau was technically the firstborn, to be the bloodline through whom His covenant promise to Abraham would be fulfilled. God determined that His covenant promises would descend from Abraham through Isaac to Jacob, "that the purpose of God according to election might stand, not of works but of Him who calls."*

[26] *Psalm 139:16 NIV*

[27] *A famous phrase from Paul Harvey's news broadcasts*

Jane At College Commencement

11

True Nobility

They are the noble ones in whom is all my delight.

Psalm 16:3 NIV

In Proverbs true nobility derives, not from royal descent, but from noble character. God says, *"A wife of noble character who can find? She is worth far more than rubies. Her husband has full confidence in her...She is clothed with strength and dignity."*[1]

Jane was this kind of a wife—fully trustworthy, noble character, spirit of excellence, shining virtues, and clothed with strength and dignity. Nine noble and regal qualities characterized her life.

Intelligence

Jane's intelligence was evident in her strong propensity for academic and scholarly activity. She loved the adventure of learning and growing in knowledge. She displayed lots of energy in her pursuit of truth.

Jane loved scholarly activities. As a Bible scholar, I have been a member of several scholarly societies. Whenever I went to Evangelical Theological Society regional or national meetings, Jane would accompany me and enjoy the scholarly papers. She was able to follow their intricate details and scholarly reasoning.

Sometimes at these meetings, I would attend one seminar topic by a certain scholar and Jane would attend an entirely different seminar that interested her. If she did not have a preference, I would suggest one. Afterwards, we would share and compare our notes. Jane loved this kind of scholarly exercise.

She was skilled and competent with Greek. Jane could research passages for me in commentaries and do as good a job as I could. If ever I fell below a high standard of excellence, she would let me know about it. In every imaginable way, she was God's gracious gift to me as a bride and helpmate.

Another example of Jane's scholarly aptitude and interests was her request to type my commentary on Hebrews, even though I had a secretary who would otherwise do the typing. Why?

She wanted to learn more about the Epistle to the Hebrews, get into the scholarly issues of the book, possibly contribute some helpful insights (which she did), plus work side-by-side with her favorite Bible scholar. Jane knew I had written my M.A. Thesis on—*A Critical Analysis of the Unresolved Problems of the Epistle to the Hebrews and Their Relation to Its Canonical Authority*. She loved a good brainy exercise and an edifying scholarly endeavor—period!

I'm still trying to comprehend how great a gift God blessed me with when He gave me Jane.

Love for the Word

Something I appreciated greatly in Jane was her firm conviction about the inerrancy and infallibility of God's Word. As a serious student of Scripture, there were things Jane found difficult to understand, facts that seemed to be contradictory, and Old Testament events and passages that she found disgusting.

But she refused to judge the Scriptures by leaning on her own understanding. Rather, she let the Word of God judge her and her sins and shortcomings. She was extraordinarily honest with her doubts and fears, but found reassurance and faith at the cross.

Her love for God and His Word grew with the passing of years. She loved His Word as pure and life-giving.[2] Did Jesus not say, *"If you love Me, keep [give attention to] My commandments?"*[3]

A couple of months after Jane's premature death at 52, I had a dream about her being at my side while I was exhorting a college class about the importance of a Psalm 119 love for God and His Word. In the dream she was so much with me that it was as if she were standing right there participating in the exhortation.

For 30 years, Jane's tenacious love caused her to stand faithfully by me. Her love for me, for God and His Word ran deep like a pure underground stream. Like Job, Jane treasured God's Word more than her daily food.[4] Because she loved God, she loved His Word. Jane's pure love for Jesus and the Holy Scriptures is one of my most treasured memories of her.

During her last two years, when her kidney function was ten percent or less, she exhorted me numbers of times about how important it was that the young generation have its foundation in the Word of God.

She said such things as—"They must know why the Bible is the Word of God and why Satan always attacks God's Word with the same line he used with Eve in the beginning: *'Has God said?'*"[5]

Integrity

Consistency and integrity were two virtues that Jane valued greatly. She found duplicity or hypocrisy repulsive. Truth and honesty were standards that she applied to herself and expected from others.

She had a profound sense of honor that was tied to biblical values. She treasured consistent integration of integrity into all spheres—physical, spiritual, intellectual and emotional. For her all spheres must be in unity with one another. This kept her alert to potential evil, sin and compromise on all fronts.

Jane was much like Daniel and his three friends in Babylon. They refused to compromise the values of their faith by conforming to culture in Nebuchadnezzar's court even at the cost of their lives. This was Jane! She might make an error in preciseness, but never in values.

If God's value system were threatened in any way, Jane would dig in her heels and not budge. She could be gentle and longsuffering for long periods of time. But if someone violated a biblical truth or moral value, she would rise up in unusual strength and resolve.

An example occurred during America's 2008 Presidential campaign. Jane and one of her longtime friends got into a discussion about Barak Obama and his campaign platform on abortion, homosexuality, and similar value issues. Jane discovered that her friend was going to vote for Obama because he was promising health coverage for everyone and she had no health insurance.

For Jane, pro-life was a moral matter that superseded other social issues. Her friend justified abortion as a political choice in the case of the poor. She reasoned that it was better to abort infants in the womb than to give birth and they be left to raise themselves on the streets.

I was in an adjoining room and heard the conversation heating up. Jane was greatly disappointed that her Christian friend of 35 years would rationalize pro-choice as an acceptable position based on social reasons, rather than going with Christian conscience and the Word of God. Jane's indignation was aroused. For Jane the discussion was about a clear black and white moral issue that, in integrity, must not be compromised.

Jane did not like debate. She was delighted when she could agree with others. She actually found all conflict and criticism disagreeable! The conversation with her friend revealed the strength of principle and integrity within her, being stronger than her dislike for debate. She would do anything necessary to preserve her integrity and stand for truth.

Wisdom

A highly educated person may have vast knowledge but little wisdom in the Judeo-Christian meaning. Wisdom and understanding, biblically, relate to the knowledge of God and the humble response of the heart to that knowledge. Scripture says wisdom is humble[6] and fears the Lord.[7] But knowledge, without wisdom and humility, puffs up.[8]

Because Jane was set apart for God at a young age, it put her on the path of wisdom early in life. When Jane's teenage peers were making foolish choices, she was submitting to God's wisdom.

Wisdom is directly related to knowledge of God, prudence, right living, humility, justice and equity, purity and mercy. Wisdom is considerate, kind, impartial and sincere.[9]

Jane understood that acquiring wisdom was related to keeping God's commandments. Acquiring wisdom and understanding are different than acquiring factual knowledge. Wisdom relates directly to loving God, fearing God and keeping His commandments, which Jane did implicitly and explicitly.

As a child, Jane loved her father dearly. I heard her say numerous times she also feared him as a child and youth. She feared him because she knew if she did something wrong, she could not hide it from him. She believed it was impossible to keep things hidden from him. Furthermore, she knew her father would hold her accountable for her behavior, precisely because he loved her.

This is what fearing God means. Wisdom understands that God will know and hold us accountable for our sinful choices with their consequences. Wisdom, therefore, avoids foolish choices and makes honorable ones.

A fruit of wisdom is honor. The older Jane got, the wiser she became. With the passing of time, it became evident she was indeed an honorable woman in all her ways. Wisdom presented her "with a crown of beauty."[10]

Jane's supreme love for God and His Word embraced wisdom as part of its treasure. She literally regarded wisdom, like Scripture, as greater treasure than silver, fine gold or precious jewels. Nobility usually treasures gold jewelry and precious stones. The nobility in Jane treasured wisdom above all these things.

Jane knew that God was her source of life and wisdom. Her love for God's Word caused her, by the Spirit, to be filled with the spirit of wisdom and revelation. Sometimes God communicated wisdom to her through a thought, a dream or a vision. She pursued wisdom as part of her passion for knowing God. Consequently, wisdom filled her heart and informed her understanding about His way of life.

Courage

Jane was a woman of uncommon courage. She had kidney failure before the age of 30, and had to have a transplant at age 32. For her to travel internationally after that was medically risky. To travel internationally with a quadriplegic husband besides, that was ridiculous. But travel we did! Jane traveled in ministry with me to Brazil for seven weeks, Guatemala for a week, Canada for a week, England for over two years, and Europe for 11 days.

Traveling and caring for a quadriplegic husband is no small thing in the United States, even when travelling in my van where we could take medical supplies and my power chair along. But the challenges go to a whole new level when flying and traveling abroad. If I had the courage to try it, Jane had the courage to assist. We did this time and time again over the years in spite of her kidney issues and my paralysis.

Another example of her courage and playfulness was an incident that occurred in a motel room. For many years Jane bathed me at home on the bed, since our home at that time did not have a roll-in shower for a wheelchair. When traveling, it was a special treat if the motel room had one. On one occasion in Oklahoma City, our motel room had a bathtub with a wide rim-edge.

Jane said, "I can help you use this bathtub."

I responded, "I don't think so. That's more than you can handle."

Jane wouldn't give it up. She pleaded, "You never get to be in a bathtub and this is a perfect opportunity. I know I can do it." She was so confident I finally conceded, contrary to my better judgment.

Getting into the tub was a challenge but doable. It's amazing the help that gravity provides. After a nice bath, it came time to get me out. As a quadriplegic, I was no help. Jane found the actual doing more difficult than she had anticipated. After repeated attempts and failures to lift me out I said, "I guess you'll have to go to the motel office and get help."

That comment was the last shot of adrenaline Jane needed. With one final effort, I landed on the top of the tub edge and was able to make the transfer out into a chair. We often laughed about this later, but at the time it was not funny. My dignity was almost crucified.

Needless to say, I never let Jane talk me into getting into a bathtub again. We later had a roll-in shower when we changed houses, which made the bathing process so much easier on her and me. These are little things that most people do not think about when they see someone like me in a wheelchair.

Loyalty

Loyalty was a major character trait in Jane. It ran deep in her. Ruth's statement to Naomi about going wherever Naomi went and not returning back to her own people, was truly Jane's heart as well.

No husband ever had a more loyal wife than Jane. She was proud of me at all times and never once was ashamed of me being in a wheelchair. To understand the measure of her love, she seldom thought of me even being in a wheelchair and was always proud to be my wife.

Like the wife in Proverbs 31, Jane was a wife whose worth was far above rubies. She was a noble woman of wisdom, strength, and dignity. As her husband, I had full confidence in her. Abraham Lincoln once said, "No man is poor who has had a godly mother." I would add that no husband is impoverished who has a trustworthy wife of noble character.

God's sanctifying grace gave Jane's love and devotion their dimension of depth. Her depth of devotion to her spouse was unusual. Her deep commitment to our marriage vows was truly inspiring.

Her expressions of affection could be subtle or overt; often they tended to be the former. In my dullness, I sometimes missed the unspoken subtle communication. This, in turn, sometimes registered for her as rejection or that I didn't care. I usually was puzzled and was slow to understand what was unfolding. These moments would then turn into deep, redemptive conversations.

Jane loyally stood at my side in every struggle or battle. She wouldn't give up when life was hard! Her loyal spirit was unwavering, strong and persevering. She courageously endured all things—because of love. As one song says, "Just don't give up, don't give in; if you don't quit, you'll win, you'll win!"[11]

Excellence

From a young age Jane manifested a spirit of excellence. I never saw her surrender to mediocrity. Whether she was singing a solo at church, playing her saxophone in the Macy's Thanksgiving Day Parade, excelling as a student, teaching her Greek Class or teaching four-year olds in Sunday School, she demonstrated a spirit of excellence.[12]

She always seemed motivated to do things well. It was not the compulsion of perfectionism but the motivation of excellence. Whether it was her unsurpassed academic excellence or some ordinary matter, quality was important to her.

This was evident in her handling of our dog, Max—a highly intelligent and strong willed Australian Shepherd. Jane took Max's intelligence as something adorable to train and his strong will as a challenge to conquer. She

Jane and Sunday School Class

bought a book about Australian Shepherds and another book on dog training.

Then she enrolled Max in dog-obedience school. They both excelled! There was something Max would not agree to, however. He agreed to be submissive to Jane, but he wouldn't submit to the teacher or lie down in the presence of other dogs.

The trainer suggested Jane train him as a personal guard dog. But Max didn't need training for that! Once our Senior Pastor was cutting up with Jane, and made a quick move toward her. In a flash, Max was in his face baring his teeth. Jane felt a special pleasure in having gained the respect and obedience of such a highly-strung and intelligent dog.

Jane demonstrated excellence and confidence as a hostess (see Chapter 21). She maintained excellence as a wife and a caregiver, and graciously insisted on excellence from other caregivers. At the present time, I have three caregivers who have taken the baton of excellence passed to them from Jane and they're carrying it well. What a gift of excellence from God Jane was!

Wholehearted

Jane's spirit of excellence caused her to be serious about her relationship with God. God warns us about being negligent or careless in the stewardship of our life. His heart is drawn to people who are wholehearted in their pursuit of Him. *"For the eyes of the LORD move to and fro throughout the earth that He may strongly support those whose heart is completely His."13* He looks the world over for people who are wholehearted in their love and affection for Him.

Jesus spoke about a whole heart when loving God. He said, *"You shall love the LORD your God with all your heart, with all your soul, with all your mind, and with all your strength. This is the first commandment."14*

Wholehearted love for God excludes the mediocrity in Western Christianity of half-heartedness, sloppy grace, and willingness to compromise with sin or give oneself to lesser pleasures. All of this is the antithesis of wholeheartedly loving God. Jane loved God wholeheartedly from a young age and it was reflected in all aspects of her life.

Serving Heart

Jane's capacity for caring and serving was amazing! When she cared deeply about a person, as she did for me all our married years, there was a very special passion that went with that. Her capacity for sympathizing and empathizing with hurting people was enormous. She genuinely enjoyed helping others.

In our generation that is characteristically me-focused and self-centered, Jane modeled the kingdom lifestyle taught by Jesus. *"Whoever seeks to save his life will lose it, and whoever loses his life will preserve it."15*

Jane laid down her life in love and service to Jesus and to me. She did whatever it took to do what was best for me. She covered me in numerous ways physically and socially that minimized other people's awareness of my paralysis.

Dottie Kane observed, "I found her to be an exceptionally caring and compassionate person. I saw how lovingly and tenderly Jane would care for Wes. She truly had a servant's heart as she went about her days looking for ways to serve her husband. She would offer comfort and encouragement to Wes in so many ways."16

Jane gave up a career and relinquished the "successful life" in order to love and assist me in my many physical limitations. She sacrificed uninterrupted sleep every night by setting an alarm to turn me in bed twice during the night. She did menial tasks that most people would find demeaning. She served me this way—not one year or five years, but faithfully for 30 years. She was my wife, my caregiver, my nurse, my physical therapist, my typist, my cook, my research partner, my friend, my confidant and my lover.

You say, "Laying down one's own life to serve others is politically incorrect." Yes, but Jesus was intentionally politically incorrect! He defined greatness entirely different than did the honored leaders around Him. And He was right! Serving brought Jane more joy and fulfillment than the world's value system is capable of producing. She was full-blooded Kingdom nobility!

---

[1] *Proverbs 31:10, 11a, 25 NIV*

[2] *cf. Psalm 119*

[3] *John 14:15 NKJV*

[4] *Job 23:12*

[5] *She encouraged me to address the following questions: (1) Is God's Word really inerrant? (2) Why and how should I love God's Word? (3) What benefits will I derive by loving and trusting God according to His Word? (4) Why should the Word of God have authority over my life? (5) What are the consequences of compromising God's Word by exalting human reason and intellect over it? (6) Why is faith in God's Word important? (7) Is the Word of God fully trustworthy? (8) What happens when my personal desires conflict with God's Word? (9) Why must the Word and the Spirit be united together at all times? (10) How can we love God and His name, if we do not love His Word and obey it?*

[6] *Proverbs 11:2 NIV*

[7] *Proverbs 9:10 NKJV; NIV*

[8] *1 Corinthians 8:1*

[9] *James 3:17*

[10] *Proverbs 4:9 NASB*

[11] *Lyrics by Misty Edwards, from the song "Turn It All Around" (IHOPKC)*

[12] *Daniel 6:3 NKJV*

[13] *2 Chronicles 16:9 NASB*

[14] *Mark 12:30 NKJV*

[15] *Luke 17:33 NKJV*

[16] *Rich and Dottie Kane are directors for the International Healing Rooms Ministries in Florida. We first met them twenty years ago when they moved from Pennsylvania to Olathe, Kansas, to be a part of our church there. Dottie developed a cancerous tumor on her left kidney and was facing immediate surgery. The Lord Jesus healed her of the tumor and her neurologist cancelled the surgery after confirming the miracle with a scope. A few years later they moved to Florida where they planted the first Healing Rooms Ministry office in a shopping center in Coral Springs. Multiple hundreds of afflicted people have been miraculously healed as a result of the Kane's ministry and that of their team. I have been honored to serve as their vice president since the ministry began.*

Jane's Alma Mater

12

College Crisis

Every branch that bears fruit He prunes, that it may bear more fruit....You did not choose Me, but I chose you and appointed you that you should go and bear fruit, and that your fruit should remain.

John 15:2,16 NKJV

A s a student, Jane knew me only as a college professor. She knew my story somewhat, but she didn't know much about my long years of preparation to get where I was when she met me. Nor did she know about God's gracious dealings with me along the way. God brought her into my life in perfect timing.

Evangelist and Revivalist

During my twenties, I was a student evangelist. My first message, at the age of 19, was at a little Free Methodist mission in downtown Oklahoma City. My first sermon was from Luke 15 on the Prodigal Son. After preaching 30 minutes, I gave an invitation for salvation. My heart leapt with joy when one man came forward.

My second time to preach was as a college sophomore during an Oklahoma City youth revival in my home church of 200 people. I preached ten messages in eight days starting on a Sunday morning. Many people—young and old—came forward for prayer or salvation. It was clear the Lord had given me both the gifting and passion of an evangelist. I burned with longing for revival and to see people get saved.

By the time Jane met me as a college professor, I had been a licensed/ordained Nazarene minister for nearly 20 years. During those years, I had preached in small churches and large, spoken in college and seminary chapels, conducted revival services lasting three weeks, numerous seven and eight-day meetings, weekend youth revivals, many Sunday services, and pastored for two years.

Jane came to know me in all these ways during our courtship and first year of marriage. Jane enriched all my life, including my life in ministry and as a college professor. At the end of our first year of marriage, I was given the *Teacher of the Year* honor at the college Awards Chapel.

Controversy

The following year, spring of 1983, a major crisis arose. I have always believed that ministry of the Word must be joined to ministry of the Spirit as in the New Testament Church.[1] The Word without the Spirit lacks life and experiential power. The ministry of the Word must be joined with the ministry of the Spirit and His gifts to be fully fruitful, a deep conviction of mine for many years.

From February 1980 to March 1983, I led student Friday all-night prayer meetings—praying for revival on campus and for our city. These prayer meetings began at 10 P.M., when campus activities were winding down, and continued through the night, sometimes till dawn. Young men preparing for the ministry, and others, were greatly impacted by God's manifest presence in these all-night prayer meetings. These young adults carried the vision of a praying church with them after college, praying for revival and spiritual awakening wherever they went.

In Acts where there is much prayer mentioned, there is also much of the Holy Spirit and His manifest presence. Among my praying students, the ministry of the Spirit increased, without teaching. The prayer meetings were led and orderly, but also characterized by freedom in the Spirit and passion. If praying in tongues occurred, something controversial in this particular denomination, it was never corporate, only personal and private.

One day the President and Vice President of the college came to my campus office and closed the door. They didn't thank me for faithfully praying with students for three years, nor for the sacrifice of time and sleep it represented. They came in like FBI agents and began questioning me belligerently about tongues. They didn't ask me whether I prayed or spoke in tongues personally, but only about my view on the subject.

I responded honestly, stating that my view was in the mainstream of New Testament scholarship and to be understood within the context of 1 Corinthians 12-14. I had never mentioned tongues during the Friday night prayer meetings.

The college president responded that if I believed this, I could no longer teach at the college. Then he told their *Teacher of the Year*, "You're fired! You are not allowed to show up for any of your classes hereafter."

How does a man tell his bride of less than two years this news? It was disturbing, but Jane handled it well. She commended me for not compromising my conscience and for standing strong with the Word of God.

I wrote a *resignation letter*. The administrators said, *"fired"*; I said, *"resigned."* I requested permission to communicate my view in a letter with all of my faculty colleagues, so they would at least know what I believed and why I was leaving the college. For me the issue was not tongues at all. Rather, it was the issue of the authority of God's Word versus religious tradition.

Pruned Back

"All fruitfulness flows from intimacy."[2] Jesus in John 15 referred to himself as the Vine and His disciples as branches that must remain in Him in order to have life and bear fruit. Moreover, every branch that bears fruit he prunes, so that it may bear more fruit.

For me the college crisis was a time of being pruned back. The pruning included my popularity and influence, my income, my insurance, my retirement benefits, my university professorship, my ego, my ministerial ordination and much more.

I had never intended to become a pastor again. As part of my pruning and for the sake of having fruit that remained, the Lord directed me to plant a new church in Olathe where I had labored six years in prayer. The church began with about 40 praying college students, many of whom were graduating seniors.

Three university administrators' paranoia about tongues caused them also to dismiss three other professors—two in the English department and one in the Speech department. The reason? Because they were close friends with me or for having sometimes attended the Friday night prayer meetings. One of the fired English professors, Mark Wilson, joined me as co-pastor of the new flock.

Our congregation had nine weddings the first summer. The Lord immersed us in Acts, prayer and community. Soon new adults were joining with us. The next four years were a mixture of exciting ventures in the Lord and fiery trials. We met in school facilities on Sunday mornings and Friday nights; we met in homes on Sunday evenings.

After our weekly Friday night prayer meetings, some of our young men and women witnessed to city youth that gathered in parking lots up and down Santa Fe, the main street of the city. Some of these youth were introduced to Jesus.

Adjustments For Jane

Jane faced many adjustments with these changes. Being a pastor's wife was radically different from being a professor's wife. Especially difficult for her was the sudden termination of relationships that happened due to our college crisis. This was painful for us both, but especially for her.

When Jane would shop at the super market, she would see people who before had been "friends," but who now would intentionally evade her by going down another aisle. This kind of rejection was something Jane struggled with for several years. God reassured her, however, that *"instead of disgrace, you will rejoice in your inheritance."*[3]

When God called me to preach the gospel, He never gave me a job description. He gave me a blank page and asked me to sign it at the bottom, with the understanding that He had permission to fill in the pages of my life and to determine what the work of the ministry would look like.

What has been my main assignment? To bear fruit! Pruning is necessary for fruitfulness. Pruning is not pleasant when it occurs. But our lives bring Him glory when we "bear fruit," "more fruit" and "much fruit."[4]

The journey is not about our comfort but about His glory! The journey of Jane and I has sometimes felt amiss, but God has faithfully fulfilled His promise in Proverbs 3:5-6 to *"make the path straight"* before me. The path, with its twists and turns, hasn't looked straight from a human perspective. But I know it's a straight course from the heavenly perspective. It's the best journey I could possibly have in this life! That's the perspective that counts for eternity.

"All is for Your Glory"
By Lisa Gottshall (IHOPKC)

There is just one chief end to man's purpose
One main reason for existence
All man's vain and high ambitions
Will one day be brought low
Will one day be brought low

For You alone will be exalted in that day
Worthless goals will be exposed as idols that we've made
For You alone will be exalted in that day
You'll be seen as rightful King and from our hearts we'll say

All is for Your glory
All is for Your name
All is for Your glory
That in all things You may have the first place
That in all things You may have pre-eminence

To treasure You above all others
To love You like we love no other
Your greatness soon will be uncovered
And all the earth will then know
And all the earth will then know

So put me anywhere just put Your glory in me
I'll serve anywhere just let me see Your beauty

My God, my Joy, my Delight

---

[1] *The ministry of the new covenant is the ministry of the Holy Spirit (2 Cor. 3:6, 8) and includes the following: 1) the initial fulfillment of Joel 2; 2) baptism with the Holy Spirit (Acts 1:5); 3) the receiving of power (Acts 1:8); 4) the Spirit of prophecy; 5) the gifts of the Spirit; 6) the fruit of the Spirit; 7) the manifestations of the Spirit and power; 8) the Spirit of freedom; 9) the anointing; and 10) the Giver of life. All the redemptive benefits in Christ come by way of the Spirit.*

[2] *Heidi Baker*

[3] *Isaiah 61:7 NIV*

[4] *John 15:2, 5*

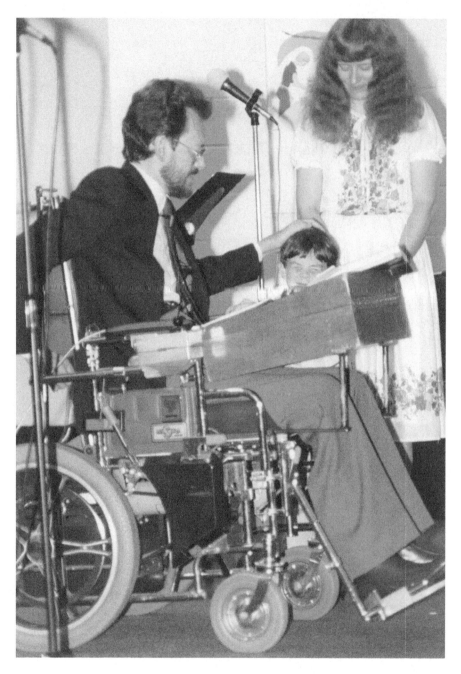

Wes Dedicating Small Boy To God

13

New Beginning

We will tell the next generation the praiseworthy deeds of the LORD, his power, and the wonders he has done.

Psalm 78:4 NIV

J ane was chosen for Who's Who in American Colleges and Universities her Junior and Senior years. Beside each student's Who's Who picture in Jane's 1980 college year book was a caption stating the student's name, college major, plus a quotation selected by the student from some famous person like Albert Schweitzer, Robert Kennedy, Albert Einstein, etc.

Beside her picture, Jane chose to place a Scripture quotation from Isaiah:

> *Do not call to mind the former things, or ponder things of the past. 'Behold, I will do something new, now it will spring forth; will you not be aware of it? I will even make a roadway in the wilderness, rivers in the desert.'*[1]

What a prophetic Scripture this proved to be in Jane's life and mine. Less than two years after we were joined in marriage, dynamic new beginnings began to spring forth!

When God closes one door, He opens another. If we are walking in faith, trust, confidence, love, and obedience as beloved disciples, a closed door will lead to a larger purpose of God in the Kingdom.

As before mentioned, Proverbs 3:5-6 has proven true in my life at every turn. As I have firmly trusted God from my heart and refused to rely on my own limited understanding, but have acknowledged and submitted to Him as Lord, He has faithfully made the path plain and straight before me.

Open Door

One year after transitioning from professor to pastor, *"a wide-open door for a great work"*[2] appeared before me. My close friend from college and seminary days, Don Stamps, contacted me about helping him write a study Bible for Brazil.

The phenomenal revival in Brazil, continuous since the second decade of the 20th century, has been mostly among the poor. Brazil's indigenous pastors, also from the poor, did not have money to go to Bible College or have a library. They had precious few resources other than their Bibles.

God gave Don an inspired idea when he and Linda went to Brazil with the Assemblies of God in 1981. The vision pertained to a study Bible that would be a library in itself for these Brazilian pastors. It would introduce each book of the Bible, providing a clear understanding of its historical context and message.

This unique study Bible would have 77 articles, two to three pages each, on important Biblical subjects placed where that particular subject is first introduced in the Bible. For example, in Genesis chapter one there is an article on Creation vs. Evolution. These 77 articles are in effect a mini-biblical theology resource.

In addition, this study Bible—later named Full Life Study Bible—would have notes at the bottom of the page explaining select verses. These notes would be exegetical, historical, expositional, devotional, or exhortational. Like other study Bibles, it would include a biblical timeline, maps and numerous other study helps.

Publishing Miracle

Don and I had graduated with honors from college, and were second and third in academic rank in our seminary graduating class. Now we were joining together to produce a strategic biblical resource for the

Brazilian Pentecostal churches, numbering about ten to twelve million people. The total project took seven years.

We began writing first on the New Testament. Near its completion Zondervan, the largest publisher of study Bibles in the world, expressed interest in seeing our manuscripts. Zondervan agreed to publish our study Bible in English. The contract made provision for the Assemblies of God to publish it in Portuguese for Brazil, and in any subsequent foreign language they desired.

This wide-open door was much bigger than either Don or I realized. The spiritual warfare that it stirred up was frightening. Every writer and editor's wife was attacked physically. Jane's kidneys declined rapidly in function; another editor's wife had to have a heart transplant. Six weeks after we completed the entire project, Don Stamps died of cancer. He was a strong and healthy man when we started the project. Though the cost was great, so has been the fruitfulness of our labors.[3]

In 2012, as I write, the *Full Life Study Bible* (original title) is now distributed under the titles of *Life in the Spirit Study Bible* (Zondervan title), and *Fire Bible* (Hendrickson Publishers/Life Publishers title).

The Study Bible has been translated into 40 languages with 28 languages waiting their turn. It is literally all over the world—North and South America, numerous countries in Europe, Asia (including Russia, China, and India), and Africa.[4]

Today I'm told that when driving in a Brazilian city, one will see believers carrying this Study Bible in their hands as they walk to church. I have seen the same thing in Times Square, New York City.

I seldom go anywhere in the world that individuals do not come up and request me to sign their Study Bible. It is reassuring when I go to sleep to know that some of my labors are at work in another part of the world where it is daylight.

Stack of Fire Bibles in Various Languages

Demotion Or Promotion?

When I transitioned from being a university professor to being a small church-plant pastor, in the natural it looked like my world was being reduced. From God's perspective, however, every step forward in His will is a promotion. If we are willing to lose our life for His sake, Jesus said we would find it. If we are willing to take Kingdom risks and be persecuted for His name's sake, He said our reward will be great.

These kinds of truths run counter to natural thinking and the ways of this world. Nevertheless, Jesus' teaching is always true and God's kingdom laws are absolute. Still, biblical truth requires faith, obedience and perseverance to walk out.

After leaving my post as a university professor, I was no longer called "Dr. Adams" every day, and no longer had a guaranteed salary with benefits like insurance and retirement. Relinquishing all of these was part of my following Jesus, crucifying my flesh, and standing with His Word.

Kingdom economics are different than men's. Jesus said that when we do these things for His sake, we lay up treasures in Heaven. In some sense, we benefit from the equity of that heavenly investment even in this life. The challenge with kingdom investment is this: the dividends are not seen in a day or even a year. It's a journey of faith; the fruit is seen only over time and in the age to come.

---

[1] *Isaiah 43:18,19 NASB*

[2] *1 Corinthians 16:9 NLT*

[3] *See biography about Don Stamps for more details of our relationship: Bob Burke, Push Back the Darkness: The Story of Don Stamps and the Full Life Study Bible (Lumina Press), 1995.*

[4] *Life Publishers, an arm of the Assemblies of God, is responsible for all foreign language editions.*

14

Please

Understand Me

*Husbands, live with your wives in an understanding way,
showing honor to the woman.*

1 Peter 3:7 ESV

Jane was a marvelously complex person and not always easily understood. First Peter 3:7 instructs husbands to live with their wives *"in a considerate way."*[1] Being considerate to one's marriage companion seems simple enough.

Peter's instruction, however, involves much more than just being considerate. A literal rendering of 1 Peter 3:7 emphasizes the real issue is *"living [with one's wife] in an understanding way"* (NASB, ESV, NKJV).

The ASV (most literal of all) says live with your wife *"according to knowledge,"* i.e., according to "intentional understanding." Then Peter adds, show her honor. Peter is exhorting us husbands to understand the unique personality and temperament of our wife in an honoring way, lest our prayers be hindered.

In one sense my assignment was difficult because Jane's personality was rare and not easily understood. Her personality makeup comprises only 1% of the population. My personality type is characteristic of only 2% of the population. Two rare and complex personalities wed together could cause a great deal of conflict and misunderstanding.

Fortunately, Jane and I discovered early in our marriage a book called *Please Understand Me,*[2] containing a very helpful personality test and analysis. Some mission agencies use this

Wes' Valentine to Jane

book to assist missionaries in understanding one another relationally, so they can better work together in ministry.

The book revealed Jane's complexities. What were some of her personality traits that stood-out?

Intimacy

Deep in Jane's heart was the desire for intimacy, the delicate sweetness of love. Intimacy has multiple dimensions—intellectual, friendship, emotional, spiritual and sexual. All these areas were important to her.

We learned to communicate and relate to one another *intellectually* at a level that few marriages do. I was always amazed at Jane's intelligence and ability to discuss all kinds of subjects in depth. Although I couldn't participate in the physical activities she enjoyed such as swimming, horseback riding, etc., we could fully participate together in the intellectual sphere. God in His faithfulness gave me a bride who fully complimented me, fulfilled me intellectually and vice versa.

Intimacy extended to our *friendship.* As both my marriage companion and caregiver, we spent more time together than most couples and therefore had more time for conversation and friendship. Jane was my best friend and we shared everything honestly from an emotional closeness. We communicated at the heart level.

We shared our *spiritual life* together—our hearts, our dreams, our most recent conversations with the Lord, and fresh revelation from the Word of God almost on a daily basis. Our love for God included a mutual strength of love for God's Word. We could study the Bible together at a devotional level or at a technical exegetical level using the Greek text and scholarly commentaries. Jane enjoyed this as much as I did.

Sexual intimacy was a greater challenge. One of my candid conversations with Jane when we were courting was about my physical limitations as a quad. Although we couldn't share the fullest extent of sexual union, God was incredibly faithful to us in this. God empowered Jane mentally and emotionally to accept this reality. Her tenacious love for me was evident in this realm also. Instead of Jane closing her heart in unfulfilled frustration, she grew in intimacy with me instead.

Jane's biggest disappointment was not sexual per se but related to her spiritual ambition, an area most wives never even consider. Like the mother of James and John,[3] Jane wanted sons who would be strong and prominent in Jesus' kingdom. Her unfulfilled dream of having strong sons for God's kingdom was disappointing and painful. Her desire physically for sons was intense, like that of Hannah, and other Jewish women in biblical times.

Jane, early in our marriage, actually felt invited by God to ask for a son who would be an evangelist like Andrew and Peter, to ask for another son who would be an intimate prophet and intercessor like Daniel and John, and yet another son with the calling and mantle of teacher and apostolic leader like Paul. She was reaching for the stars in an intercessory way. Even though her dream was frustrated in the physical realm, God did give us strong spiritual sons for the kingdom over the years in each of these categories.

Sentimental

Jane was a Home-Sweet-Home person. Her home was her castle. Normally she would rather be at home than anywhere else.

I remember the year we made a six-week ministry trip to New York and the East coast. As we pulled out of our driveway, Jane began to cry.

I asked her, "What on earth is wrong?" I was exhilarated at the thought of a six-week trip. She was depressed because she didn't want to leave home and pets behind. Once we got into the trip, her adventurous side kicked in and she thoroughly enjoyed it. But getting her away from home was always a challenge.

Jane's sentimentality ran deep. For example, it was unthinkable for her not to be at her parent's home in Wamego on Christmas Eve singing Christmas carols, reading the Christmas story in Scripture, drinking alcohol-free wassail and having fun with the family. The strength of this sentiment became evident a few days before Christmas in 1983, our third Christmas as a married couple.

Ten days before Christmas I had presented a paper at the Evangelical Theological Society's annual meeting, that year in Dallas. After the ETS meeting, Jane and I drove to Brownwood, Texas to visit my parents.

She insisted that we must leave Texas and get back in time for Christmas Eve in Wamego. With this pressure in mind, we left Brownwood on December 23rd about 6:00 A.M. It was the coldest December 23rd probably in the history of Texas—6° above zero at Brownwood.

Normally Brownwood is so mild that residents do not cover exposed pipes under the house. My parents had no central heat, only a little gas heater in the living room. That morning as Jane dressed me, the temperature in our bedroom was in the 40's.

Not only was the cold severe, there was a thick layer of ice between Brownwood and the Oklahoma border. Until we got there, I drove very slowly with my passenger-side wheels on the gravel shoulder in order to have a little more traction. We saw cars in the ditch everywhere, some of them overturned. The van heater was inadequate, and the driving tedious and nerve wracking.

At the Oklahoma border, the highway was 100% snow-packed. The highest temperature we saw all day was 10°. Driving continued to be hazardous. We repeatedly saw cars and trucks overturned in the ditches. It was dark when we reached the Kansas border, with ever-increasing amounts of snow and plummeting temperatures. But we "had to be" home for Christmas Eve in Wamego, Kansas.

By the time we reached Wichita, the gas line was starting to freeze. I pulled into a service center, and left the van running while Jane ran in to buy containers of HEET for the gas tank. After adding several, we continued on our way through the blizzard.

Between Wichita and Kansas City, we saw an overturned semi-truck and later learned that the driver had died. But we "had to be" home for Christmas Eve in Wamego. Had our van stalled, we both could have frozen to death. We drove into our Olathe driveway about 10:00 P.M. with it still snowing and 10 below zero.

The next morning I awoke with the sorest and stiffest neck as a result of the 16-hour drive in life-threatening weather. Because of my neck and the severe cold temperature that dropped to 20º below, we were unable to be in Wamego for Christmas Eve or Christmas Day. What a hard lesson learned! Sentimentality cannot be permitted to lead.

Jane's sentimentality included love for her pets. She always had a dog and a cat and would have had multiple dogs and cats had I agreed. She wanted a pet bird, but I could never come to peace with that thought. She fed the neighborhood birds and squirrels. As if she didn't have enough responsibilities already, she wanted to have an aquarium with fish to constantly clean and feed—which she got. This feature in Jane was totally beyond me.

Humor

Jane could be intensely serious, yet she could also be hilariously funny and roar with laughter. She brought me much joy with her mischief, wit and humor. People loved watching this aspect of our relationship. She was a gift to my heart and to those around us.

Many young adults have stayed overnight with us across the years. Many more have lived with us during our 30 years of marriage. All of them alike loved Jane's mischievous playfulness and would be overcome with laughter at her fun-loving ways.

Our good friend of many years, Dottie Kane, remarked about Jane's sense of humor:

> She would brighten up our times together with her witty stories. She had a way of sharing that would bring about within you a joyful and a merry heart. There were times that we would laugh so much that tears would roll down our faces.[4]

Jane loved clean and playful humor. Her wit and humor were spontaneous. One way she enjoyed engaging in humor was by word associations, play on words, and the subtleties inherent in words.

Her favorite cartoon strip was Calvin & Hobbs. The author, through little Calvin's personality, constantly made fun of Calvinism and other philosophical views and issues. She would roar with laughter at the subtle innuendos. If she were reading it by herself, when she found a really juicy one, she would bring it to me to share her joy.

Jane's favorite spoof of religion was *The Mississippi Squirrel Revival* by Ray Stevens. This hilarious song is about a boy who caught a squirrel and brought it to Sunday church in a shoebox. When attempting to show his friend, the squirrel got loose and went berserk in the morning service in Pascagoula, Mississippi.

Jane's vivid imagination could see every bit of the story live and in color before it went visual on YouTube.[5] Her laughter was animated, vivacious and contagious.

Jane loved genuineness and could recognize a phony a mile away. *The Mississippi Squirrel Revival* is a parody about the hypocrisy of some self-righteous church people and the controversial external manifestations that occur in a genuine revival atmosphere. As the song's lyrics say, "Some thought it was Heaven; some thought it was Hell." None of that was lost on Jane. Her humor was both intellectually complex and childlike in fun.

Jane's favorite movie was an obscure one, *The Mouse That Roared,* with Peter Sellers playing multiple roles. It was therapeutic to watch this movie with Jane and hear her laughter. It was more fun than the movie. She was great with children because of her love for Veggie Tales, Wallace & Gromit, Sean the Sheep, and the Pink Panther.

Jane laughed many times about a humorous incident that happened to me in my wheelchair. One summer I decided to re-seed our front lawn after a hot, dry summer. After re-seeding, the new seed needed to be watered twice a day until the seed sprouted and put down roots. One area between the sidewalk and curb was too small for a lawn sprinkler, so I watered it by hand from my wheelchair.

Our house was on a corner lot, with the yard bordering on the busiest residential intersection in Olathe. The four-lane street on one side of our house was a thoroughfare and downright dangerous. While watering near this intersection during rush hour traffic, one of my wheels pulled the hose out of my hand and the sprinkler sprayed directly into my chair's brain box (circuit board).

Bad things happen when water and electricity try to mix, even in a battery-powered wheelchair. At that moment my chair went berserk, completely out of control! My directional joystick no longer responded as the chair moved entirely on its own. I turned the power switch off, but that didn't matter either. It kept on moving wildly with my wheels throwing mud in every direction.

Eventually my front wheels went over the curb, leaving my back wheels spinning off the ground. I wrapped my arms around the chair's handlebars so not to go out on my head. I was yelling at the top of my voice.

Fortunately Jane heard me and came running, only to see my back wheels still spinning and throwing mud in the air. My chair had made a mess of our newly planted grass, but at least it hadn't gone out of control into the busy rush hour traffic a few feet away.

Jane shouted, "What are you doing to our yard?"

"Never mind what I'm doing to the yard! Help!"

Finally my wheelchair motor stopped running. "Pull me back to the sidewalk!"

Jane disengaged the gears and pulled me back to the sidewalk. I then explained to her what had happened. She didn't believe a chair could move on its own. In her unbelief, she re-engaged the gears and turned the switch on—and away I went, completely out of control, going in circles and tearing up the yard even more and further jeopardizing my life.

Jane looked surprised that this really was happening. Though I immediately turned off the switch, the chair continued to spin wildly in circles until it eventually stopped again.

At this point I spoke forcefully to Jane—"do not touch that switch again!"

The scariest part of being out of control was the intersection. Had the chair gone toward it, I most likely would have been hit by the fast-moving traffic.

Many people have "cracked-up" over this story, including Jane. But the consequences were not funny! Technicians were never able to make the chair function correctly again. I had to get a new wheelchair.

Temperament

Jane was finely tuned like a violin. She had a deep and intuitive sensitivity that caused her to be reserved, even a bit shy. Because people could easily hurt her, she tended to be a private person.

Yet Jane also could be extremely warm, exciting and engaging with those she knew well and trusted. This was true with young and old. Young adults would sometimes sit and talk with her for extended periods of time because she was so interesting and engaging. Her eyes would be alive and dance with pure joy when she was fully engaged.

She was a superior listener and could get on my case for not listening carefully. She flourished when she felt like she was being listened to and her words were valued. Because her words were purposeful, she felt devalued when people didn't listen or value what she had to say. Like most of us, she was not immune to the desire for approval.

Whenever someone treated her rudely, tempting her to push back with unkind words or emotions, she would guard her heart. The exceptions to this were rare. She typically thought of the other person's well being, not just her own.

Jane and I regularly hosted a home group. She was sensitive and alert to the needs of everyone present. If someone were uncomfortable, she would offer that person her chair, if it were an improvement. If someone needed a glass of water, Jane would be the first to recognize that. Many evenings she would sit on the stairs to make sure others had a seat. Her awareness antenna caused her to be alert to others in the group at all times. Sensitivity can be a positive asset in relational dynamics, not just a negative one.

Above all else, Jane was sensitive to what God thought or said about issues that she faced in life or in her heart. She was always resolved to please God above pleasing herself or others. Her sensitivity to God was extraordinary. In this she was always an example of a godly woman.

Breadth and Depth

Jane was able to understand complex issues and people. She could hold her own in a deep theological discussion with men, plumb the depths of C. S. Lewis, or talk about flowers and cooking with women. Her life clearly had the dimensions of breadth and depth, a treasure house.

Her range of interests was broad. She stimulated me spiritually and intellectually, often contributing ideas to the content of my teaching and preaching. She was a constant inspiration to go further and reach higher for more of God.

Jane loved beauty and simplicity, and devoured Thoma Dubay's book, *The Evidential Power of Beauty*. Dubay argues that the whole realm of beauty speaks of the character and nature of God. Jane was deeply attracted to the beautiful because she was greatly attracted to God.

She loved beautiful flowers, beautiful scenery and the beauty of God's creation. She was especially fond of England because of the beauty of its quaint villages and countryside, the peaceful scenes of sheep grazing in a meadow, the tall hedges and roses lining little country lanes in Cornwall, and England's majestic cathedrals.

She loved reading the spiritual classics and the contemplative authors in church history. She was attracted to C.S. Lewis and the breadth of literary genre in his writings.[6] If C.S. Lewis liked certain writers and was influenced by them, then Jane would like them too and read them—e.g., George MacDonald, J.R.R. Tolkien, G.K. Chesterton, etc. These writers all had a way into her heart that pulled her deeper into God. She collected books by all of these men and was enriched by them.

Jane was a prolific reader. In 2004, Jane read 52 books. Unlike Max Lucado, whom she enjoyed reading, many of these books were heavyweights. For example, that year she read four of G.K. Chesterton's books, a number of books on Saint Francis of Assisi, C.S. Lewis on *The Four Loves,* Francis de Sales' *Authentic Devotion,* Charles Ringma's *Resist the Powers with Jacques Ellul,* and Bernard Bangley's *Near to the Heart of God.*

In addition to 52 books that year, Jane read the entire Old Testament twice; read the entire New Testament four times. She also read the

Gospel of John 10 times and the entire book of Acts 10 times. That's a whole lot of reading in one year!

She was a person who felt things deeply. I was challenged constantly to understand her personality. Some of the challenges were typical male/female issues. But my challenges went far beyond the ordinary. Jane would say hers went far beyond the ordinary too. The more I grew in my understanding of her, the more I loved her and thanked God for the splendid multifaceted gift she was to me and others.

Inner-Life

Jane had a rich inner-life and inner-strength that came from her relationship with God. Dottie Kane remarks:

> So many times when Wes and Jane were staying at our home, I would find Jane reading the Word of God. She loved the Lord and His Word. She had a great spiritual depth to her that would emerge in conversations we had together. She loved to get into theological discussions that would uncover truths that were hidden in God's Word.[7]

Jane had a strong faculty of introspection and reflection that enabled her to think deeply and meditate on the Word effectively. She appeared at times to be mystical. She was generally very reserved and did not share her inner life except with a few persons she really trusted.

Jane had a sensitive conscience, far from those who have a calloused conscience from repeated exposure to sin. She had a prophetic capacity, which the Holy Spirit used again and again.

Special Gifting

Jane was highly intuitive. She was gifted with dreams, visions and supernatural experiences that were easily misunderstood by people who lived only out of the natural mind. The Holy Spirit would speak to her through auditory and visual images.

Like Joseph and Daniel in the Bible, Jane was a prophetic dreamer. The Lord gave her profound dreams and visions. She had a hard time trusting her ability to hear God correctly through the inner voice of the Spirit. So the Lord would often communicate with her through images in dreams and visions, which made great impact on her spirit.

She had an uncanny ability to know my thoughts and to communicate on a level that superseded words. Jane could be aware of another person's emotions or intentions even before the person was conscious of these. Many times she would know what I was thinking or what I was going to say before I said it.

She stewarded her ability carefully with wisdom and a pure heart, never using it manipulatively or for personal advantage. She sometimes used it with me playfully. She used her gifting in a way that others would be unaware that a special gift was being engaged. Jane didn't like being a visible leader, but she did enjoy quietly exerting influence behind the scenes.

Vivid Imagination

In addition to having a great mental faculty, memory and intuition, Jane had a vivid imagination. This is one reason she related well to children and young people. Her imagination was so keen, it had to be guarded and protected.

When she was young, she was introduced to horror stories and books on witchcraft. These stories not only scared the daylights out of her, they haunted her for years to come before she found complete deliverance and freedom from them.

The enemy succeeded for a while in associating the Holy Spirit with ghosts, especially when preachers used the King James vocabulary of the Holy Ghost. For years she was a bit apprehensive about the Holy Spirit and His manifestations because of the ghost stories in her childhood.

At the same time she was intrigued and curious about the Spirit's gifts in a way that was refreshing. Her keen interest in the Holy Spirit began in high school and continued through the years.

Jane's extraordinary imagination, intuition and literary gifting drew her to poetic literature. She sometimes composed complex songs and poetry herself.

I have been immeasurably enriched and deepened in my own walk with the Lord as a result of having her by my side for 30 years. May God raise up a new generation of godly women who are set apart by God for His pleasure and glory.

[1] *NIV 1984 ed.*

[2] *David Keirsey, Please Understand Me II: Temperament, Character, Intelligence. Prometheus Nemesis Book Company, 1998.*

[3] *Matthew 20:20-28*

[4] *Dottie Kane and her husband Rich are directors of the International Healing Room Ministries in Coral Springs, Florida.*

[5] *Google for a YouTube visual dramatization.*

[6] *Mark Wilson, an English professor at Mid-America Nazarene University, introduced Jane to C. S. Lewis through classroom instruction.*

[7] *Dottie Kane, Coral Springs, Florida*

Hungry For More Of God

15

"More, Lord"

As the deer pants for the water brooks, So pants my soul for You, O God. My soul thirsts for God, for the living God.

Psalm 42:1-2a NKJV

In January 1994 a revival visitation began at Airport Vineyard Fellowship in Toronto, Canada, that impacted spiritually thirsty believers of many nations for a decade. Revival services, called the "Toronto Blessing," ran day and night for years. People from all over the world by the thousands encountered God and the presence of the Holy Spirit there.

The revival was characterized by unusual phenomena such as "holy laughter," weeping, involuntary bending, groaning, shaking, and falling (called "slain in the Spirit"). These unusual manifestations were clearly from the Spirit's presence and power, not religious quackery or fleshly emotionalism.

Jane and I visited these revival services for five days in November 1994. The manifestations of the Spirit we saw were an amazing sight! Nearly everything we saw has occurred before in historic revivals all over the world, including the Moravians, John Wesley's meetings, the preaching of George Whitefield and by Jonathan Edward's own wife, Sarah, during the great awakening.

Jane was so impacted by the Spirit at Toronto, and her desire for more of God was so great, she did something very unlike Jane. She flew back to Toronto in the spring of 1995 for a second revival visit without me. It was the only time in 30 years she flew somewhere without me. Such was her thirst for more of God.

The signature cry of the revival was, "More, Lord!" The desire of the human heart for more of God and more of His Spirit was powerfully reproduced over and over again in people from various nations when they visited the revival site. When Jane and I went to England in 1995-96, evidence that the Toronto revival had migrated to England was present in London and everywhere we went. During the first year of the Toronto revival, all flights from London to Toronto were full daily and had to be scheduled a week to ten days in advance. The cry—"More, Lord"—was intense!

Jane's Journey

For Jane, the journey for more of the Spirit began years before when one of her high school teachers, a charismatic Methodist, conducted a Bible study for students in the basement of Jane's home. He taught on the baptism in the Holy Spirit, the gifts of the Spirit, the fruit of the Spirit, etc. A biblical foundation was laid for Jane to understand the Holy Spirit and His ministry worldwide today.

Jane was never passive about truth, especially God-truth. This was evident during a summer Christian youth camp attended by Jane, Julie Meyer and "the Roth twins," good friends of Jane—each from Wamego High School. Jane was a senior; Julie was a freshman.

The youth camp doctrinally believed the supernatural gifts and manifestations of the Holy Spirit were not for today. From past camp experiences, Jane knew they believed the Spirit's supernatural gifts ceased after the New Testament was completed.

During the first camp session, Julie, a new Christian, had her paper and pen in hand, ready to take notes on everything said. Jane told her, "If the speaker says something that's not true, I'll kick you and you'll know not to write that down."

The speaker read Acts 2:4—*"All of them were filled with the Holy Spirit and began to speak in other tongues."* The speaker paused: "Not everything in Acts 2 is for today. Speaking in other tongues is not for today." Jane gave Julie a KICK and she stopped writing.

The speaker read further, coming to Peter's words from Joel 2—*"I will pour out my Spirit on all people. Your sons and daughters will prophesy, your young men will see visions, your old men will dream dreams."*[1]

"Christians today are filled with the Holy Spirit when they get saved and Christians today do not speak in tongues" [KICK]. The speaker continued, "Christians today do not prophesy" [KICK]. "Therefore, young men and women no longer prophesy" [KICK], "no longer see visions [KICK], and no longer have prophetic dreams" [KICK].

Julie told me this story at Jane's memorial service. She added, "The next day I literally had a bruise on my leg from Jane's signals."

Today Julie Meyer is a musician, worship leader and songwriter at the International House of Prayer in Kansas City. She's known the world over for her prophetic songs, visions and prophetic dreams as in Acts 2. As a teenager, Jane demonstrated an ability to discern and stand for truth, making sure the camp speaker did not deceive Julie. What a good outcome!

My Journey

My journey in the Spirit began my first year in college. When I read about Jesus' ministry in the Gospels, I was struck by how prominent healing was in His ministry and how seldom it is mentioned or practiced in the church.

After reading Leonard Ravenhill's book, *Why Revival Tarries,* I understood more why the great chasm exists between the New Testament church and the contemporary Western church. When I studied Acts, a deep longing for more of the Holy Spirit in my life occurred repeatedly.

In February of my sophomore year, Owen Murphy, an international evangelist, came through Oklahoma City, telling about the great Hebrides Revival and exhorting the American church to pray for revival. That night an impartation of fiery intercession for revival entered my innermost being.[2] That flame of the Spirit has not ceased to burn within me with passion, desire and intercession for more of God.

Jesus placed great emphasis on the importance of the Holy Spirit's presence and power. Immediately before His ascension, Jesus instructed the twelve, and eventually the 120 who joined them, to collectively wait in prayer in Jerusalem for a full encounter with the Holy Spirit.[3]

Jesus' first disciples knew that life in the Spirit was essential. They were filled with the Holy Spirit's presence and power as Jesus promised.[4] In demonstration of the Spirit's power, they proclaimed the testimony of Jesus effectively—first in their city, then in the larger region, and finally to the nations.

To participate fully in Jesus' strategy for fulfilling the Great Commission, we must encounter the Holy Spirit and His supernatural gifts to empower us for the task. Our assignment from Jesus is to proclaim the gospel of the Kingdom with the Holy Spirit's anointing, just as He proclaimed the gospel of the Kingdom with the Spirit's anointing.[5]

As a seminary student, I came to realize that apart from more of the Holy Spirit, I was very limited as His witness. I read David Wilkerson's classic, The Cross and the Switchblade. I told God I wanted to know Him and the ministry of the Holy Spirit in this kind of dimension, not the limited measure with which I was presently familiar.

My good friend Don Stamps and I continued to hunger and thirst for more of the Holy Spirit. Our seminary senior year, we made an appointment to meet with the senior pastor of the First Assembly of God in Kansas City. We'd heard Brother Grant was especially effective in laying hands on and praying for the baptism in the Holy Spirit. That evening in his office, both Don and I were baptized in the Holy Spirit and made our plunge into the deep.

The Spirit and Brazil

Two years later, Don, his wife and small son went as missionaries to Brazil with the Nazarene denomination. Within a year or two, a huge crisis arose. The denomination's top tier of leadership sent a mandate to the Nazarene missionaries in Brazil to question all indigenous Nazarene pastors whether they prayed or spoke in tongues. If they did, the missionaries were required to remove these Brazilian pastors from their churches if they refused to renounce their experience in the Holy Spirit.

Don and Linda, with four other Nazarene missionary couples, refused to comply and were brought back to the United States as a result. Eight years later, Don returned to Brazil with the Assemblies of God and with the vision of writing a Spirit-filled study Bible for the vast Pentecostal revival of that nation and beyond.

God affirmed Don's refusal to compromise his conscience or the Word of God concerning the Holy Spirit. God gave him the freedom and the platform to influence positively the revival in Brazil, one of the biggest nation-wide revivals in history.

Word And Spirit

Jane and I took our congregation on a corporate journey into life in the Spirit. Four years after leaving the university, this journey in the Spirit led us to join our congregation with the work of a young Spirit-filled leader named Mike Bickle whose ministry was exploding in Kansas City. Mike was devoted to prayer and fasting for revival. As a leader, however, he also led his congregation into a lifestyle of prayer for revival and life in the Spirit.

The Lord blessed his leadership so that six different congregations affiliated with him in the city. Our congregation in Olathe merged together with two other local streams to become one of the six congregations. We bought a skating rink and converted it to accommodate large gatherings.

This congregation grew rapidly to about 500. As one of the pastors, the church gave me freedom to work on completing the *Full Life Study Bible* project that Don and I had begun three years before. This was an ideal situation for me, enabling me to continue hands on ministry as I devoted myself to writing.

After completing the *Full Life Study Bible*, I started survey classes of the Old and New Testament for six Kansas City congregations and anyone else who wished to enroll. There was such a hunger for this kind of biblical study that Mike started Grace Training Center, a three-year Bible college.

This school fully embraced the integration of the Word and the ministry of the Holy Spirit. In fact, we had a School of the Word and a School of the Spirit. The latter had classes on prophetic ministry, gifts of the Spirit, healing and deliverance, dreams and visions, etc.

A few years earlier I had been forced to leave a university by leaders who resisted integrating the ministry of the Word and Spirit. God, in His faithfulness, then opened the door to write a study Bible that fully integrated the Word and the Spirit. Then He opened the door for college-level teaching again that fully integrated them both.

There's More

Jane and I came to be greatly challenged by the level of Kingdom authority and power demonstrated by a contemporary missionary in Mexico. As in Jesus' ministry and that of the early Church, the level of spiritual authority and power in David Hogan's ministry is clearly greater than ours. This confirmed our belief that there is much more authority and power of the Spirit available today than we are presently experiencing in the Western church.

God has worked through Hogan and his team in Mexico to raise more than 450 people from the dead. We tend to rationalize when someone dies, *"it was just his or her time to go."* The death of these 450 dead in Mexico could have been attributed to "their time to go" and then religiously buried. Instead, a missionary and his team took Jesus' words seriously and pulled 450 people from the jaws of death—by the power of God.

Without question we have watered down Jesus and the gospel to fit our comfort zone. Listen carefully to Jesus' words to His disciples, *"As you go, preach, saying, 'The kingdom of heaven is at hand.' Heal the sick, cleanse the lepers, raise the dead, cast out demons. Freely you have received, freely give."*[6]

Jesus also said less than 24 hours before His death, *"Most assuredly, I say to you, he who believes in Me, the works that I do he will do also; and **greater works than these** he will do, because I go to My Father. And whatever you ask in My name, that I will do, that the Father may be glorified in the Son. If you ask anything in My name, I will do it"* [emphasis mine].[7]

As I've been writing this week, a 17-year-old Hispanic boy was gravely injured in a car crash in Kansas City. About 40 family and friends gathered at his bedside as he lay in a coma with serious head injuries. Some of my team members shared the gospel with the family and prayed for a miracle. They did this several days in a row before the young man died.

What a perfect context for a *sign* miracle. Most of those involved didn't know the reality of Jesus Christ. But the miracle didn't happen and he died! That evening I went to Jane's grave and grieved my own lack of spiritual authority and power to heal the sick and raise the dead as He commanded.

This is one reason I spend hours in the prayer room crying out for more of the presence and power of the Holy Spirit in ministry. Jesus raised the dead! Peter and Paul raised the dead! David Hogan raises the dead! "God, why are we not raising the dead—neither in the mortuary or the pew?"

Having wrestled with this issue for years, I know well the tension between trusting God as in *the rest of faith* and the pull of the Holy Spirit to press on until I attain *"to the whole measure of the fullness of Christ."*[8]

This is part of the radical edge of intercession for transforming revival that God put in our hearts. Jane felt so strongly about this, she urged me to have special Sunday night services in England to stir intercessors to take hold of the greater works that Jesus promised to His church.

Keep in Step

"Those who are led by the Spirit of God are sons of God."[9] Normal Christian living is life in and by the Spirit!

God has always done His work through the presence, power and activity of the Holy Spirit. Even Jesus always did His ministry through the presence and power of the Holy Spirit. No person on earth, not even Jesus, can do the work of God without the Spirit of God.

The early church always did ministry, just like Jesus, through the presence, power and activity of the Holy Spirit. Paul concludes in Galatians 5:25, *"Since we live by the Spirit, let us keep in step with the Spirit"* (NIV).

---

[1] *Acts 2:17 NIV*

[2] *My book,* The Fire of God's Presence, *tells about my encounter with Owen Murphy and describes supernatural scenes from the Hebrides Revival, including Murphy's own miraculous deliverance from polio and healing of paralysis.*

[3] *Lk. 24:49; Acts 1:4-5, 8*

[4] *Acts 2:1-4*

[5] *Isaiah 61:1; Luke 4:18*

[6] *Matthew 10:7-8 NKJV*

[7] *John 14:12-14 NKJV*

[8] *Ephesians 4:13*

[9] *Romans 8:13-14 NIV*

Bless our God, O peoples,
let the sound of his praise be heard,
who has kept us among the living,
and has not let our feet slip.
For you, O God, have tested us;
you have tried us as silver is tried.
You brought us into the net;
you laid burdens on our backs;
you let people ride over our heads;
we went through fire and through water;
yet you have brought us out to a spacious place.

--Psalm 66:8-12 NRSV

16

Comfort In Affliction

This is my comfort in my affliction,
Your word has given me life.

Psalm 119:50 NKJV

J ane was a person of strength. She was strong in spirit, mind and soul, and even strong in body. Yet mysteriously she experienced kidney failure. Her doctors were never able to determine why. It was first discovered during the summer after she graduated from high school.

Red Flags

Before starting college, Jane was diagnosed by her primary care physician as having a kidney infection. The problem baffled her Wamego doctor, so he sent her to a hospital in Topeka, Kansas for a thorough exam.

The specialists at Saint Francis Hospital never communicated clearly with Jane or her parents about the potential seriousness of her kidney issue. Jane thought it was simply a passing infection and she could go on with life as before. In retrospect, we know this was the first sign of a kidney disorder that eventually led to kidney failure.

The second red flag occurred when Jane went for her physical exam before we got married. This doctor noted there was an abnormal amount of protein in the urine that should be carefully watched. Again the communication was poor. There was no reason offered or instruction given on how to proceed.

The third red flag appeared when Jane had only 20% kidney function left. Oftentimes kidney failure is a consequence of diabetes or some other disease. Jane had no disease. Her kidney failure mystified her doctors.

Furnace of Affliction

Daniel's three friends in Babylon were not delivered from the furnace experience; instead Jesus joined them in the furnace. Jane was not delivered *from* the furnace of affliction, but Jesus definitely joined her *in* it.

At the onset of Jane's kidney decline, she was thrown headlong into the furnace. Before her kidney decline, the only physical affliction Jane had known was an occasional sinus infection accompanied by headaches. Now Jane developed high blood pressure and hypertension headaches that had to be controlled by drugs.

After her kidneys failed completely, she was placed on peritoneal dialysis, with overall declining health following. She carried 2.5 liters of fluid in her stomach area, requiring her to wear loose clothing. Otherwise she looked about seven months pregnant.

After 18 months of dialysis, Jane had her first kidney transplant. She later had three additional surgeries—one to remove an infected appendix with gangrenous tentacles; another to remove her angry gall bladder; and eventually a second kidney transplant.

Jane suffered intensely from both the appendix issue and the gall bladder before they were removed. Having a transplanted kidney required suppressing her immune system with drugs. One of many side effects from these drugs was a sharp increase in her cholesterol. When her doctor prescribed cholesterol medicine, on two separate occasions, Jane's liver became severely toxic, causing her great weakness and exhaustion.

Another side effect of her drugs was degenerative cartilage in her feet and knees. This likewise caused her a great deal of pain up to the day she died. In the end the furnace of affliction was intense.

Original Shock

Five years after we were married, Jane, at age 28, began having weekly incapacitating headaches. She would vomit violently and be left without strength. We prayed earnestly that God would heal the headaches and their cause. We had no clue what the root problem was.

During a seven-week editorial assignment in Brazil (1987) with Don Stamps working on the *Full Life Study Bible* and living with the Stamps' family, Jane's headaches were especially severe. The headaches were so incapacitating at times she would have to crawl to the bathroom in order to vomit.

When we returned from Brazil, I took her immediately to an excellent Christian doctor. When the nurse took her blood pressure, it was 220 over 144. The nurse said, "Lie down and remain still." We now had an answer—her terrifically high blood pressure was causing her headaches.

The next step was to determine what was causing the abnormal blood pressure. The doctor's diagnosis was solemn but not final. He referred us to a nephrologist, a kidney specialist.

Grim Diagnosis

The nephrologist did further blood tests. He and his nurse then came into the little room where Jane and I were waiting. I remember how grim they both looked, especially the nurse.

Dr. Husemann spoke bluntly, "Jane's kidneys are failing and there's nothing I can do to stop it. She has only 20% kidney function left." Then he confidently predicted, "After about eighteen months, she'll have to go on dialysis to clean her blood or she will die within a matter of a couple of weeks."

When I heard these words, my soul went numb. I wept bitterly for three days. Jane was actually more composed than I was. It was incomprehensible to me that this was happening to my bride, the gracious gift God had given me only a few years before.

Our pastoral team strongly supported us in prayer and provision. Intercessors prayed earnestly for healing and restoration. Yet after 18 months, Jane's kidneys completely failed.

Jane was given a choice between two types of dialysis: 1) hemodialysis, or 2) peritoneal-dialysis. The former is done three times a week at a dialysis center. The patient is hooked up to a machine for 6-8 hours and all of the blood's impurities are removed.

The peritoneal method involved an exchange of fluid through a catheter into the peritoneal chamber next to the stomach. This could be done at home. Jane chose this method so that she could be at home more to assist me. Nevertheless, the schedule was grueling. She had to exchange fluid in the peritoneal chamber four times a day. She was thinking more about me than about herself, a distinctive feature of her character.

Jesus in the Furnace

St. John of the Cross wrote, "O living flame of love that tenderly wounds my soul in its deepest center!"[1]

When Jane was in the hospital to have a peritoneal catheter surgically inserted, Jesus appeared at her bedside and gave her His arm. She knew this meant she would have to go through this season, but He would walk with her.

The old peritoneal dialysis method was a poor substitute for kidneys. During the next 18 months impurities gradually accumulated, affecting almost all her physical functions. She lost weight, her hair looked dead and fell out and her countenance was ashen gray. One of my colleagues later remarked, "She looked like walking death."

One way Jesus was with Jane in the furnace was through the precious people He placed around her. A team of prophetic intercessors met with her several hours each Thursday evening over the 18 months. They prayed and listened for a word from the Lord. Their ministry to Jane was life sustaining—spiritually and even physically.

---

[1] *St. John in "Stanzas the Soul Recites in Intimate Union With God."*

17

Joy Comes In The Morning

Weeping may endure for a night,
but joy comes in the morning.

Psalm 30:5b NKJV

Dr. Diedrich, head nephrologist at Kansas University Medical Center in Kansas City, introduced us to the idea of a kidney transplant and what would be involved. Jane and I prayed about this for months. We didn't want to act out of fear or out of a lack of faith.

Finally we had peace about putting Jane's name on a list of transplant candidates. She was tested for blood and tissue type, antibodies, and three other categories. All six categories are determining factors in a good transplant match.

New Year's Day

A qualified transplant candidate often has to wait for a year or two. Jane's wait was seven weeks! The phone awoke us from our sleep at 7:00 A.M. on New Year's Day 1991. Jane answered and heard the head nephrologist's voice, "We have a kidney available if you wish to receive it."

We learned that a ten or eleven year old boy had accidentally shot himself in the head while examining a friend's older brother's gun.

After a few days in the hospital, the young boy died and his parents donated his organs.

I asked Dr. Diedrich whether it mattered that the donor was male and that he was so young. He said the gender didn't matter and a young kidney from a healthy child was the best of all possible options. People who had been on the transplant list much longer were passed over in favor of Jane because she was such a good match. She was young, 32, and the donor was young.

After answering all our questions, Dr. Diedrich, added that they needed a decision by 8:00 A.M. If we chose to receive the kidney, we would need to be at KU Medical Center by 9:00 A.M. The first thing that went through our mind was, *this is not very much time to make such a serious decision and it's impossible to be there by 9 a.m.*

It was impossible because Jane would have to do a dialysis exchange, shower, then assist me with personal needs, dress me, get me out of bed, pack a suitcase, and get on the road for a 25 minute drive. Normally this would take a minimum of two hours.

The first thing we did was to call our close friends and intercessors, Mike and Linda Laughlin. Being early New Year's morning, we awakened them as the doctor had us. They agreed to pray and see if they could hear anything from the Lord. Jane and I prayed together as well.

Our friends put a pot of coffee on to get awake enough to pray. They had one strong impression, "It's more right to go for the transplant than not to." That seemed right to us as well.

Time Miracle

How Jane did everything necessary in such a short time, we may never know. As we were driving to the hospital suddenly God gave me a flood of understanding and assurance that this transplant provision was from Him. We were able to go through the whirlwind of that day with peace that we were in God's will and that He was with us.

When we checked in, it was only 9:15. They prepped Jane for surgery and I scrambled to enlist caregivers to assist me in her absence.

The year before Jane's kidneys failed, we had extraordinary grace from the Lord. Angels came to our house in the night and Jane had a supernatural grace to live in the Word of God night and day. She read the Bible for hours at a time receiving revelation and life flowing into her.

When a church member learned what was happening with Jane's Bible reading, she asked Jane to lay hands on her and pray for an impartation. Jane did and she received it!

The moment Jane's kidneys failed and she went on dialysis, God seemed distant and a foggy memory. For Jane it was the dark night of the soul. It was the most difficult part of her whole experience—this seeming distance and silence of God.

Kidneys control many strategic physical functions. But as we painfully learned, kidney failure affects every dimension of one's life—emotional, mental, physical, and spiritual. Her spiritual fogginess was related to the failure of the kidneys themselves.

Yet in this "dark night of the soul" was the hand of God that *"causes all things to work together for good to those who love God, to those who are called according to His purpose."*[1]

Transplant Miracle

The news traveled quickly through our church and there were over 20 intercessors at the hospital when they rolled Jane from the prep room toward surgery.

My father was present and he stopped the whole procession and announced, "We must all pray first." A prayer meeting occurred in the quiet hallway of KU Med Center on that New Year's morning when most people were recovering from the night before or preparing to celebrate a new year. For Jane and me, it was not only a new year, but also a new kidney and new beginning.

Jane was moved to the ICU for the night. She was groggy from the sedation and didn't remember me being there. However, her parents and grandmother came in immediately after me, and Jane recognized them and spoke to her grandmother. This was significant because it was the last time Jane saw her grandmother alive. I said goodbye and went home without her for the first time since we were married.

The next morning Jane was sitting up in bed, very alert, eyes clear, and color returning to her countenance. The moment I saw her, I knew I had my precious Jane back.

Post-Surgery

Jane's recovery was slow but steady. There were some brief, nerve-wracking setbacks such as a temporary rejection episode that required her to return to the hospital for a few days.

Also Jane's blood pressure continued to be high and difficult to control, even with drugs. This perplexed her doctors, since a kidney transplant normally brings blood pressure back to normal.

In addition to recovering from surgery, Jane's body had to adjust to heavy doses of immuno-suppressant drugs to keep her body from rejecting the foreign organ. Gradually the dosages were reduced to a low maintenance level.

One of these drugs was Prednisone, which caused her to gain weight and gradually changed Jane's face to a more round shape. She struggled, as anyone would, over this change in her appearance. Ironically, this was one of the less serious side effects of the drugs she was required to take for 20 years.

As the young kidney bonded and functioned efficiently, new vigor and life returned to her. All the accumulated impurities were cleansed. A revival of health and a measure of youthfulness returned.

But her spiritual life was slower to recover. The message of worship songs seemed unfamiliar to her at first, and the Bible was dry and unfamiliar. The good news is that Jane did experience a spiritual revival. Worship again ushered her into God's presence and a place of intimacy. Much like Job, her life in God was deeper and richer as a result of the fiery trial of her faith.

---

[1] *Romans 8:28 NASB*

18

Hope And Glory

The LORD reigns, let the earth be glad;
let the distant shores rejoice.

Psalm 97:1 NIV

One of the academic disciplines in high school that Jane greatly enjoyed was English Literature. Among her many English interests were British history, English culture, and English poets and their literature. From the time she was a small girl, she would read stories and novels about England. She even had a curious interest in Sherlock Holmes, evidence being her having read all his books.

Jane's father was Swedish but her mother was largely English. Jane dreamed and longed to visit England and live there. Eventually, the Lord gave her the desires of her heart.

Brits Come To Kansas

England is called "the land of hope and glory" for several reasons—natural and spiritual. Spiritually it has a rich revival heritage. Many of the great hymns of the church worldwide were written there during England's times of great revival.

The expression "the sun never sets on the British Empire" was once not only a political and socio-economic reality, but also a spiritual one. Wherever the British Empire extended in the world, it became a network for the spread of English culture and missions.[1]

Beginning in 1987 our congregation had an amazing sequence of three pastors with British roots and accents. The first one, *Noel Alexander,* was from South Africa where British culture and an adapted English accent predominate among Caucasians. He had an eloquent British accent and a prophetic edge.

David Ravenhill followed. He is the son of the famous Leonard Ravenhill—a powerful revivalist from England. David also had a distinctive British accent and was a good preacher and teacher.

David Miller, an English pastor from a church in Peterborough, England, followed Ravenhill. Miller pastored our Olathe congregation for three years and then returned to his congregation in England. He highly esteemed my teaching abilities and wanted me to come to England to join him in ministry there.

FIRST ENGLAND TRIP

After considerable encouragement from Jane, we went to England for two weeks in June of 1995.

Our first visit was exhilarating and packed full each day. I was never so alive with history as during those two exciting weeks. We made numerous trips out from Peterborough. We visited historic sites in

London, Oxford and Cambridge Universities, Ely and Peterborough Cathedrals, and Epworth, where John Wesley was born, raised, and preached on his father's tombstone when expelled from the church building. We succeeded in getting Jane to climb up on the tombstone shrine and pose as if preaching—it was truly cute.

In London we saw the normal tourist attractions—Big Ben, Parliament, Westminster Abbey, Saint James Park,

Smith Wigglesworth gravesite, England

Buckingham Palace, 10 Downing Street, St. Paul's Cathedral. But I especially wanted to see two spiritual landmarks: 1) Westminster Chapel (pastored sequentially by G. Cambell Morgan, Martin Loyd-Jones, and R.T. Kendall), and 2) John Wesley's Methodist Chapel, home and burial site.

John Wesley Center

Next to John Wesley's chapel (the mother church of Methodism) was his very modest home—quite small but straight up four floors. I wanted to see John Wesley's bedroom, the bed in which he died and his study/library. These were on the third floor and accessed only by a very narrow stairway that made perilously sharp turns.

In England I had to be in a manual wheelchair, instead of my normal motorized chair, because of transportation issues. We first stripped down my chair by taking the leg and foot rests off. Then my friends, Wes and Jono Hall,[2] carried me in the chair up the stairs where I almost got stuck on one of the turns.

For a moment I thought I might become one of the permanent furnishings in this historic home. Visiting Wesley's little bedroom where he went to be with the Lord was a holy moment. But it was his study/library where I most wanted to spend time.

I requested the opportunity to be in that study alone for fifteen minutes. My request was granted and I had a most unusual encounter with the Lord during those minutes. I cherish it to this day.

Afterwards, I rolled to the third floor window that overlooked the busy London street. Across the street was the famous cemetery where Susanna Wesley, Isaac Watts,

John Wesley's Home in London Squeezed in Next to His Church

John Wesley's Study, London

John Bunyan, and many other famous, English saints are buried. I saw David Miller and Jane returning from the cemetery. I was overwhelmed with gratitude for the goodness of God in making this all possible.

Church Highlights

Our connection with the saints at Church on the Rock in Peterborough was truly remarkable. This host church received us as if we already had a long history together. A very special love-bond was made with the congregation during our two weeks.

The two weeks with Church on the Rock involved preaching four times on the two Sundays, meetings with leaders and individuals, eating dinners in several English homes, developing many new relationships and establishing enduring friendship with the saints in England.

Jane and I flew back to Kansas City very tired, but also very happy and grateful to the Lord God for such an exceptional experience of His favor.

SECOND ENGLAND TRIP

With great joy Jane and I returned to England the next summer (1996) for two full months. David Miller fully prepared the Peterborough congregation for our return visit. Our reception by them was nothing less than royal.

During these two months, I taught courses on Revival and on the Book of Acts, ministered the Word in the congregation, and interfaced with the five leaders of the church on numerous occasions collectively and one-on-one. I also met with leaders from other congregations and cities, and preached in one of three historic Baptist churches that sent William Carey as a missionary to India.

Bishop Cox

Jane and I both had many roots and spiritual heroes in England. Some of Jane's English ancestors came from Olney where John Newton, composer of Amazing Grace, pastored and is buried.

My Adams clan was from England, Wales, and Ireland. My grandmother Adams, also English, had an ancestor named Richard Cox who was Bishop of Ely Cathedral in the 1500's.

The Anglican Cathedral of Ely was only about 30 miles from Peterborough and was one of the first places we visited during our previous trip. An inscription over the big cathedral doors read—"Prayer has been offered to Almighty God in this place since A.D. 1300."

Ely Cathedral, Cambridgeshire, England

My ancestral grandfather, Bishop Cox, is buried in the floor of the cathedral and a plaque is mounted on the wall in his honor. He was a biblical scholar, taught at Oxford and Cambridge, translated Acts and Romans for the *Bishop's Bible,* and was a tutor for King Henry VIII's only son, Edward VI.

I learned of my blue-blood connection, interestingly, just before our ventures in England began. My very first "preach" in England was in the Ely diocese where Bishop Cox resided. I thought this was somehow significant.

Village of Elton

Our host congregation obtained a small house for us during the two months in a quaint English village[2] where lots of doctors and lawyers lived. Jane was a little awestruck, thinking she and I would be out of place.

The Crown Inn in Village of Elton, England

Jono Hall, however, assured Jane that we were aristocrats in England. The three professional occupations most esteemed in England are medical doctors, lawyers, and professors. Having a Ph.D., and being a college professor, moved us up several rungs on the social ladder from our lowly status in Olathe, Kansas.

The quaint village of Elton was idyllic, located 7 miles SW of Peterborough. Peterborough, England was a city of 200,000 population (80 miles North of London). The big picture window in our Elton bungalow looked out over a grassy meadow where sheep sometimes grazed peacefully. Beyond we could see the church spire in the village of Fotheringhay 5 miles away where Mary Queen of Scots was executed. Famous history in England is everywhere.

Our home base in Elton was a hub of all kinds of Church activity during our two months. We entertained leaders, hosted youth groups, Sunday potlucks and even a surprise 55th birthday party for me.

From Elton we made significant trips to London, Charles Spurgeon's Tabernacle, Oxford, Cambridge (numerous trips), Ely, Thrapston, Bristol, George Mueller's orphanage and Wales.

My teaching ministry that summer on Acts and on Revival greatly impacted many lives for which we give God glory and thanks. Certainly our roots in God and in England went deeper those two months.

---

[1] *The lyrics of the song called "Land of Hope and Glory" encapsulates England's "glory days." This patriotic hymn is sung in England to the tune of Pomp & Circumstance. Some of the words are as follow: Land of Hope and Glory, Mother of the Free, How shall we extol thee, who are born of thee? Wider still, and wider, shall thy bounds be set; God, who made thee mighty, make thee mightier yet! / Truth and Right and Freedom, each a holy gem, Stars of solemn brightness, weave thy diadem. / Hearts in hope uplifted, loyal lips that sing; Strong in faith and freedom, we have crowned our King! // To this day, this national hymn is sung at all kinds of events in England—soccer games, rugby games and big gatherings of any kind. Most Englishmen will throw back their heads and sing it with all their lungpower. It is truly inspiring to be in England and hear them sing about their nation as "a land of hope and glory".*

[2] *The first Sunday dinner Jane and I had in England was with Jim & Jessica Hall and their four children. These precious people became like family to us. At the time, Wes was a law student at Bristol University and Jono was just finishing high school and later did a degree in Law as well. Both Wes and Jono, and their families, now live within minutes of me and are strategic leaders in the International House of Prayer of Kansas City.*

[2] *The village of Elton is located approximately 7 miles (11 km) south-west of the city of Peterborough in Cambridgeshire county, England.*

God's Oil

For The Sake Of The Nations

19

Anointing In England

With my sacred oil I have anointed him.

Psalm 89:20 NIV

The very first Sunday morning I spoke in England was a most unusual service. After reading the Scripture and before I could begin my first message, evidence of the Holy Spirit's presence began. Youth in the service had open visions of God's power and glory coming to England. One teenage girl, a first time visitor, had never had a vision from God but did that morning. After the service she shared with me what God had shown her. Neither before nor since have I seen such a service.

Another teenage girl, Elizabeth,[1] had a vision of a pierced hand holding a pitcher and pouring golden oil. The vision was so vivid, she drew what she saw (see previous page) and gave it to me, feeling that it related to what God was doing that morning.

Preparation

Preparation for our two years of ministry in England (1997-1999) began early in February and March of 1997. I was on a long, extended fast during which the Lord spoke to me about taking a sabbatical and going to England for at least a year.

God graciously gave me details about how and what I should do to make this possible. The instruction was comprehensive and included transitional issues concerning my job at Grace Training Center; renting our house; providing for my parents who were in their 90s; and other details such as how to ship my converted van to England so that I could be mobile with both my van and power chair during the two years.

Leaving my parents in Olathe to go abroad was a huge concern for me, as they were still living by themselves. The Lord assured me that He would take care of them while I was gone.

It was with great anticipation that Jane and I returned to the land of the John Wesley anointing. We arrived in England for our two years a couple of days after Princess Diana's funeral. The entire nation was in mourning. People's hearts were tender.

OUR FIRST YEAR

Our years in England were nothing short of phenomenal. They were among the happiest and most fulfilling years of our married life and ministry. I helped David Miller, the senior pastor, put an infrastructure in place for Church on the Rock. This included selecting and training leaders at every level.

Soon after arriving, ironically I, an American, trained English leaders for doing the British Alpha Course. The Alpha Course, a very effective relational form of evangelism, subsequently became this church's most effective outreach and discipleship ministry. Many people have been saved through it and added to this church over the years. The church's overall infrastructure and core leaders are still in place today. It was a busy, but fulfilling and fruitful two years.

Europe

After nine months, Jane and I made an 11-day ministry trip to mainland Europe. An intercessory friend of ours from Kansas City, Carol Hoffmeier, flew to England to accompany us.

We traveled across France and spent some time with former students in Basel, Switzerland. While there, I visited Basel University where two of my New Testament professors did post-graduate studies under the famous theologians Karl Barth and Oscar Cullmann.

The next day we drove to Lucern, Switzerland, where I preached in the first public service of a new Vineyard church, planted by three of my former students. While in Switzerland, we also had opportunity to visit

Langnau, the community where my mother's people lived before immigrating to the USA in the 1840s. We also visited places like Bern, Zurich and Appensell.

In addition to Switzerland, we visited six other European nations. When crossing the border into Austria, we encountered some carry-over bitterness from World War II. The Austrian armed guard was rude and gruff when he discovered I (the driver) was an American. He pointed at my GB (Great Britain) sticker on my van and barked "Verboten!" (Forbidden!). He made me remove the sticker and throw it in the trash before permitting me to enter.

The border guard's intense hostility was like a dagger in Jane's spirit. It frightened her, but didn't dampen her love for the movie musical "The Sound of Music."

We also visited Lichenstein, Germany, France (including Strasborg), Luxembourg and Belgium (including Brussels & the EU^2 Headquarters). In all these places I asked God to send revival from heaven. Then we returned to Calais, France, where we put the van back on a hovercraft to return across the English Channel.

When we disembarked at England's port-city, Dover, famous for its white cliffs, Jane was greatly relieved to be back where people all spoke English. For her, England felt like "home sweet home."

Kansas City

Between our first and second year in England, we returned to Olathe for about six weeks to take care of pressing business that included again renting our house for the second year.

When we arrived, I learned that my father was ill but had refused to go to the doctor until I returned. He had to be admitted to the hospital and died 11 days later. This was shocking, but I was grateful that we were there for this intense time for dad and mom.

In addition to this crisis, the Lord told us to sell our Olathe house, not rent it as during the first year. We extended our time back a few weeks to make sure my mother was taken care of and to hopefully sell our home before returning to England. We signed the papers just an hour before driving to the airport, not knowing where we would live when we returned next time.

OUR SECOND YEAR

While we were in England an amusing incident occurred related to Chinese Checkers. Jane grew up winning table games because her grandmother always let her win. Then I came along.

As an athlete, I was fiercely competitive. Thankfully, God has tempered this. But Jane disliked my competitiveness when playing Chinese Checkers.

I fundamentally don't like being a loser. And I seldom ever lost playing Chinese Checkers. Whether two, three or six people were playing the game, I would win. Other players tried to copy my strategy but would get lost in all the moves and I would win. If just Jane and I were playing and I won, she would be provoked. But if multiple people were playing and I won, she was proud of her husband.

Then the inevitable happened in the home of an English family. After dinner they suggested we play Chinese Checkers. They had heard Jane tell of how she could never beat me. Several people were playing that night.

When all marbles had made the journey to their destination, Jane had beaten me. She was ecstatic! Even the host family joined in the celebration of my downfall. After that night, Jane could never say again with integrity that she didn't like competition.

Revival Focus

During our two years, we visited Wales, Scotland and all parts of England. Everywhere I went in the UK and Europe, I claimed territory for God, for His kingdom and for genuine revival. We poured a bottle of olive oil over the white cliffs of Dover and prayed for revival to engulf that part of England and Europe.

Jane and I poured oil and prayed for revival at Land's End in Cornwall overlooking the Atlantic Ocean, praying for S.W. England and America. At Carlisle, in N.W. England, we poured oil by the River of Eden in the local park and prayed for revival to restore what the locusts had eaten.

At Newcastle in the northeast, one of the three main revival centers of John Wesley, we poured oil on the steps of the Anglican Cathedral on a Friday afternoon during rush hour traffic. With three other intercessors, we prayed at the top of our lungs for revival to shake again that city for God.

Finally, we poured oil on John Newton's grave. This site is geographically central England. We prayed there for revival in the Anglican Church as the spiritual heart of the nation.

Pentecost Weekend

On Pentecost weekend, May 1999, I spoke four times within 24 hours at an Anglican renewal center near Worcester in western England. Carol Oosthuis, an anointed worship leader of Dutch/English decent from South Africa, led worship. Five Anglican vicars attended, but the weekend was largely a lay renewal conference. The presence of the Lord was awesome.

The night the conference ended, Jane read Carlos Anacondia's chapter on healing before lying down to sleep at 1:30 A.M. She was quickened in faith to ask for healing for her shoulder, feet, and kidneys. When she awoke Sunday morning, her left shoulder was healed and never troubled her again. Why were her feet and kidneys not healed? God only knows! But we were so grateful for the healing of the shoulder.

After the last service, Jane felt I was to pray for Carol Oosthuis. I prophesied to her about harp and bowl (worship & intercession) and a coming increased anointing in these two areas.

At the time, I was wearing a sweater that had the emblem of the globe with various flags from the nations encircling it. Above the flags was written, "Kansas City," where we had just bought a house with the money from the sale of our Olathe home.

After praying, I said, "Carol, the Lord has given us a spacious house in a suburb of Kansas City. If God directs you to come to Kansas City, you can stay with us."

Two months later, Jane and I returned to Kansas City. Two weeks after our return, Carol came to live with us.

Fond Farewell

Our church in Peterborough was full of prophetic intercessors. These precious people faithfully prayed and fasted for Jane and me to be healed during our years among them (1995, 1996, 1997-99). They petitioned God to heal me in England, before we left the end of July 1999.

Some have not stopped praying for us over the years. Their love and affection remain strong, and our spiritual bond has endured the separation. I am eternally grateful for the fruitful years and treasured memories I have in "the land of hope and glory."

We left part of our heart in England. It's a sad reality to know that Jane will not be at my side if I minister in England again. My years there were the time of my greatest anointing in ministry. I'll be surprised if I do not return. Lord God, send powerful, transforming revival with signs and wonders to England and the U.K. once more before Jesus returns.

When Jane and I arrived back in Kansas City on August 4th, we went straight to my mother's little retirement apartment in Olathe. She was overjoyed to see us again after ten months. She was ninety-four and frail, but still clear-minded, very courageous and living by herself. When we came through the door, her eyes lit up. She had lost my father one year before after fifty-eight years of marriage and had lived the last ten months alone. I arrived home five days before she had a double stroke.

Before the stroke occurred, we had Sunday dinner with her. She dressed up in her Sunday best, looked like a doll and was so happy to have us back. When I arrived Tuesday A. M. at the ER, a stroke in the early morning had incapacitated Mom so she couldn't speak and didn't ever recognize me again. It broke my heart.

I was by her side in the hospital reading Scripture aloud when her pastor, Rev. Charles Pickens, came into the room. Charles and I had been classmates in college and good friends ever since. I spoke to him about my mother with deep emotion—

> *"Charles, there was never a day of my life that I was not bathed in the prayers of my dear mother. Her prayers followed me around the world. The years I was ministering and preaching in England, she faithfully interceded for me. In fact, my mother faithfully prayed for me my entire life."*

What an eternally sacred memory! She died eleven days later and awoke in the presence of Jesus.

---

[1] *The daughter of Jim and Jessica Hall; sister of Wes, Jono, and Justin. Married to Sam Douthwaite.*

[2] *European Union*

IHOPKC Praying For Wes & Others

20

Night And Day

Prayer

One thing I have desired of the LORD, that will I seek:
that I may dwell in the house of the LORD all the days of my
life, to behold the beauty of the LORD, and to
inquire in His temple.

Psalm 27:4 NKJV

Three years into my university teaching, some students preparing for Christian ministry saw my passion for revival and requested that we pray together for a campus revival. What followed changed my life forever.

Friday Nights

When Jane and I began courting, I had been leading Friday night prayer meetings on campus for three months. Friday night on most college campuses is "party night," not "prayer night." But on this campus, Friday night was "prayer night" for some students and one professor.

The first "all night" of prayer started at 10 P.M. and continued until 6 A.M. with campus-wide participation. God endorsed it from the beginning. Thereafter for three years, after a full week of teaching, I would go home, take a nap, and then return to the campus for a night of prayer beginning at 10 P.M.

On these nights I learned about the enlarged effectiveness of corporate intercession for revival versus individual prayer. My prayer for revival previously was largely individual, mainly because there were no others around me whose hearts burned with desire to pray for revival.

After three years of Friday nights of prayer, God began birthing corporate intercession for revival on a city level in Olathe and Kansas City that went deeper and broader.

This fire of corporate intercession now burns brightly, not just on Friday nights, but 24/7 with the International House of Prayer of Kansas City (IHOPKC) under the leadership of Mike Bickle and an army of worshippers and intercessors. I have the privilege of being part of this around the clock worship and intercession 365 days a year. In 2012, as I write, IHOPKC has completed 13 years of non-stop 24/7 prayer.

Importance Of Corporate Prayer

Before His ascension, Jesus instructed His disciples to remain in Jerusalem until the Holy Spirit was poured out. The 12 rallied 120. *"These all with one mind were continually devoting themselves to prayer."*[1] Their persistence in prayer together for ten days made the outpouring of the Holy Spirit possible on a large scale.

United, corporate prayer is not optional! It is absolutely necessary if another classic, historic revival from heaven is to occur globally and in the fullness that God intends at the end of the age.

Jesus said, *"Men always ought to pray and not lose heart,"*[2] indicating we will lose heart and wane spiritually if we do not pray. This underscores the importance of corporate prayer. Churches that are not praying together become lukewarm. Prayer is the spiritual atmosphere required for spiritual life and passion to be sustained.

A few decades after Ephesus experienced the greatest spiritual awakening of any Gentile city in the first century,[3] Jesus said to them, *"You have left your first love."*[4]

The flame of love requires intimacy with the Beloved. Love burns with desire and longing for the one loved. God has this longing and desire for us, and He has placed longing and desire in us for Him. It must have expression corporately or the flame of love will flicker and go out.

The foremost way love and intimacy is cultivated is by spending time with the one loved. Worship and prayer help keep the flame of our first love for Jesus burning. For this reason we are instructed, *"Pray without ceasing."*[5]

Jane and I learned at the beginning of our marriage, the urgency of personal prayer and corporate prayer for sustaining the flame of the Lord. This reality is best learned in actual practice, not in books. The Lord taught us this lesson through all-night prayer meetings on a college campus and subsequently in our church plant.

Wisdom Of Prayer

Mike Bickle, an apostle of prayer, came as a young visionary to Kansas City in December 1982. He started a congregation that prayed together six evenings a week from 7-10 P.M. I had never heard of a church doing this before and was fascinated by his bold leadership in prayer.

The place of prayer is the place of intimacy with Jesus and revelation from the Holy Spirit. The more we pray corporately, the more we grow corporately in Christ by understanding God's heart, God's Word, God's Spirit and God's ways.

A corporate journey is a slow one. A person can travel much faster alone than with others. But God wants us to make the journey together as the Bride of Christ. In so doing, fruit comes forth that will remain.

Jane and I saw corporate prayer working in England. Our church in England had corporate prayer meetings 6-8 A.M. Monday through Friday, followed by a very simple breakfast together. This provided a marvelous fellowship opportunity and debrief-time following the two-hour prayer meeting.

The Holy Spirit's life flourishes in His people when they pray and share faith together. Where there is much prayer, there will be much of the Holy Spirit. The converse is also true: where there is little prayer corporately, there will be little evidence of the presence and activity of the Holy Spirit corporately.

IHOPKC Begins

Mike Bickle started the International House of Prayer of Kansas City (IHOPKC) in May 1999, initially functioning 18 hours a day. In September 1999, this House of Prayer began a 24/7/365 schedule that continues to this day.

When Jane and I arrived back from England in August 1999, Mike was appealing for people to serve as worship leaders and prayer leaders during the early morning hours of 3-6 A.M. This was a difficult time slot to fill and one remained open on Sunday mornings. Not wanting to be left out, Jane and I signed up to lead the Sunday 3-6 A.M. set.

In order for us to do this, Jane had to start getting me up at 1 A.M. in order to be there at 3 A.M. After the three-hour prayer meeting, Jane and I would have breakfast and then attend the Sunday morning service. In the afternoon, after taking a brief nap, I would prepare to teach for three hours on Sunday evening.

This schedule was far too demanding for Jane and me to continue forever, but it was a good experience at the outset of IHOPKC's night watch that now includes a "Fire in the Night" internship.

When Stuart Greaves, Director of IHOPKC's "Fire in the Night", took over our 3-6 A.M. shift, I told him my Sunday morning slot was special because those were the hours during which Jesus was raised from the dead. He later told me this observation inspired him to persevere during those last three Sunday morning hours of an all-night prayer vigil.

Houses Of Prayer

Jesus declared, when cleansing the Jerusalem Temple at the beginning and near the end of His earthly ministry, *"My house will be called a house of prayer."*[6] Immediately after, *"the blind and the lame came to Him at the temple and He healed them."*[7]

When the church again becomes a house of prayer, she will again become a house of healing where Jesus heals all manner of disease and infirmity. Extraordinary prayer always precedes extraordinary visitations of God among His people. When God's house is no longer a house of prayer, His presence withdraws to a distance and the supernatural manifestations of His presence cease.

God is re-emphasizing in this century the priority of prayer. Houses of Prayer are springing-up in cities and nations worldwide. In Jerusalem alone, a city with a population of approximately 850,000, there are eight Christian Houses of Prayer, some being 24/7.

In addition, multiple hundreds of Jews and Gentiles pray daily at the Wailing Wall, the very wall of the former Jerusalem Temple courtyard where Jesus contended for God's house of prayer. No wonder Jesus declared, *"My house shall be called a house of prayer for all nations."*[8] He added, *"ZEAL FOR YOUR HOUSE WILL CONSUME ME."*[9]

The House Grows

One of the joys of my life has been to watch the 24/7 House of Prayer in Kansas City grow. From dawn to dusk and through the night, through all holidays (including Christmas), prayer and worship continue 24 hours a day, 7 days a week, 365 days a year. Here prayer is not a fad, it's a lifestyle!

Large numbers in the Prayer Room are young adults. Worship and prayer mingle together as an incense offering that rises to God's throne night and day. Many prayers are for revival and spiritual awakening in cities, nations and all spheres of society. One often senses angelic presence and activity in the prayer-sanctuary, and in the small "healing rooms" around the perimeter.

Charisma magazine featured IHOPKC in the fall of 2010. This positive article highlights the miraculous way in which 24/7 prayer and worship is attracting the younger generation, both in the USA and around the world. Other magazines and newspapers have covered this spiritual phenomenon, including the *New York Times* and *Los Angeles Times*.

God TV and the IHOPKC Media bring the prayer room in Kansas City into homes in 200 nations. A 24/7 live webcast enables thousands of intercessors hourly to connect with the large KC prayer furnace in places like Egypt, Israel, Iraq, the Middle East and nations the world over. Closed nations are connecting so that few remaining nations are isolated from the reality of night and day prayer.

Fire Of Love

A prophetess named Anna, a widow in her 80s, served God with fasting and prayer night and day in the Temple. Not surprisingly, she was filled with revelation and spoke of the Messiah to all those who looked for redemption in Jerusalem.[10] Revelatory understanding flourishes in the place of prayer and fasting.

Mary of Bethany is a picture of the flame of love. Her heart was so captured by love for Jesus, she poured an expensive fragrance over His body as a love-expression. Because she valued spiritual intimacy with Jesus, she was willing to "waste" her life on Him—all because of love!

A broken generation is now responding to Jesus' invitation to love and intimacy with Him in the context of 24/7 corporate worship and prayer. Like Mary Magdalene, who loved much because she was forgiven much, this generation is also learning to love much because they are forgiven much.

The fire of love is more powerful than any other motivation. When love burns with affection for the Father and for the Lord Jesus Christ, it is not only pure, but also powerful in its redeeming impact.

God is changing the understanding and expression of Christianity in this generation. In the context of night and day worship and prayer around the world, forerunner messengers are being raised up globally. They are preparing the way of the Lord, motivated by the fire of love, by heralding the full prophetic message of the Lord Jesus to the nations before He returns.

The Bride of Christ will be comprised of young and old, rich and poor, people of every ethnic and cultural background—with one great, common feature. This multi-faceted Bride, all redeemed by the blood of the Lamb, will worship and adore Jesus from the overflow of great love for all eternity.

---

[1] *Acts 1:14*

[2] *Luke 18:1 NKJV*

[3] *cf. Acts 19*

[4] *Revelation 2:4 NKJV*

[5] *1 Thessalonians 5:17 NKJV*

[6] *Matthew 21:12-13; John 2:12-25; cf. Isaiah 56:7*

[7] *Matthew 21:14 NKJV*

[8] *Mark 11:17 NKJV, et. al.*

[9] *John 2:17 NASB*
[10] *Luke 2:36-38*

Sign Beside The Adams' Front Door

21

Trinity House

And all those who had believed were together and had all things in common. . . . They were taking their meals together with gladness and sincerity of heart.

Acts 2:44, 46 NASB

"All human beings are made for life in community with God."

C.S. Lewis

One feature of the Jesus People Revival in the late '60s and early '70s was the partial rediscovery of the Acts 2:42-47 experience of Christian community. I was impacted by that revival and its message about Christ-centered *koinonia* (Greek for Spirit-created "fellowship").

The Lord placed a strong desire in my own heart for true Christian community and *koinonia* as a result of the Jesus People Revival. I felt God gave me a measure of revelation concerning the significance of community in Acts and for the end-time church. I often prayed the Lord would permit me to have a house where biblically sound community could be cultivated and experienced.

Grandview

Though we heard God say, "sell your [Olathe] home", we had no idea where we would live when we returned from England. Jane and I committed that to the Lord and trusted He would make it clear in His time.

Before returning to England for our second year, we attended a birthday party at a house in Grandview. About six weeks later, our friend Carol Hoffmeier contacted us in England that this particular house was now for sale.

Grandview, Missouri is built partially on the old Truman farm where President Harry Truman grew up. This small suburb, located on the south edge of Kansas City, has a population of less than 30,000.

The city founders called it Grandview because it sat on high ground and provided a "grand view" to the West. Two of IHOPKC's campuses are located in Grandview. We believe that because of 24/7 worship and prayer, this little Missouri town is destined to become a "grand view" of the kingdom!

I didn't remember much about the house for sale in Grandview except that the living room had a peaked ceiling that reminded me of a little chapel or an A-frame Swiss chalet. The living room also had a floor-to-ceiling brick fireplace with large vertical windows on each side that looked out through a large oak tree to the 14th fairway of a golf course.

The house had three levels and was ideally located for my teaching at Grace Training Center when I returned from England. After praying, Jane and I expressed our interest. But could we, while living in another country, buy a house we hardly remembered except for one room?

As our interest in the house grew, we asked Diane Bickle, Mike's wife, to check this house carefully for us concerning its soundness and suitability for a wheelchair. Diane had helped us sell our house in Olathe. She gave us a thumbs-up. Carol Hoffmeier and the house owner put together 82 photos of the house inside and out, along with a cassette narration of each room.

We laid it all before the Lord again. One of my concerns was the house size. Why would we need such a large house? It would be a lot of work for Jane to maintain. The Lord answered: "You'll rent rooms, which will help sustain you in the days ahead."

Jane and I bought the house. The sale of our little house in Olathe nearly paid for the bigger house we were now buying in Grandview. The Olathe home was in one of the most expensive counties in the USA; Grandview happened to be on the other end of the spectrum. Ironically, the

Grandview house is nearly three-times larger, six years younger, better built, and in a quiet subdivision on a golf course, unlike the heavy traffic on our noisy corner in Olathe.

Trinity House

It was customary in England, particularly in the village of Elton where we stayed, to name one's house or cottage. We decided to do the same with our house in Grandview.

Since it had three levels, we named it "Trinity House"—the top level representing the Father, the middle level where our master bedroom was located representing the Son, and the lower level representing the Holy Spirit. The house was located on a semi-circle street with a nice English name, having about 22 houses and separated from the main traffic flow in the sub-division.

Carol

The first person to live with us at Trinity House was Carol Oosthuis from South Africa. As before mentioned, during a Pentecost weekend conference in England, I told Carol that if the Lord led her to come to Kansas City, Jane and I wanted her to live with us.

Unknown to Jane and me, Carol had been asking the Lord for direction and had expressed a desire in her heart to come to Kansas City to Grace Training Center where I taught. By the time Carol got back to South Africa, the Lord had spoken clearly to her about coming to live with us.

Two weeks after Jane and I returned to the United States from England, Carol stood on our front porch in Grandview with two suitcases and $300, the sum total of her belongings.

This was a God arrangement from the beginning! Carol proved to be an absolute joy to us from that day to this. She became like a precious daughter. It was certainly a God-moment on Top Barn Farm in England when we connected and prayed over her.

Carol now lives about two miles from Trinity House with her husband Wes and four lovely children [a forth child, Seraphine, was born since the picture below]. From the beginning she was an important part of ministry at the International House of Prayer in Kansas City. Her husband, Wes Hall, was a lawyer in London with a large, prestigious law firm when IHOPKC started. A year or two after Carol came to live at Trinity House and became part of the 24/7 "Prayer with Worship" ministry in Kansas City, Wes left the big law firm in London. In response to God's call, Wes discontinued the practice of law to become an intercessor missionary and end-time forerunner messenger in Kansas City. Wes and Carol were married on 7 July 2001 in Newcastle, England. After a honeymoon to South Africa (Carol's original home), they returned to Kansas City as the new home of them both.

Wes & Carol Hall Family With Wes - 2011

Lindsay and Esther

The second person to join us in Trinity House was Lindsay from Dallas, Texas and almost immediately followed by her friend, Esther.

These three young ladies in our home created a whole new learning curve for me.

The first winter our furnace went out on the coldest day of the year. Jane built a fire in the living room fireplace, and Carol and Esther slept in front of it. Every hour or so, Jane would get up, take care of the fire, step back over Esther and come back to bed in our un-heated bedroom. Lindsey had it the best. She had a space heater in her room and stayed reasonably warm through the night. Fortunately, a one-year warranty bought at the time we purchased the house covered the cost of a new furnace.

Another interesting memory with these three girls was the New Year's Eve night ushering in the year 2000. All the fright stirred up by the media over Y2K was in the air. All along I had made fun of it, but the girls and Jane made sure we had a large supply of water and food, etc. When the New Year came in with no wrinkles whatsoever, my voice gained additional authority in the house.

Community

The Lord truly gave us *koinonia* as a house of peace. Over the last 14 years, we've had 60-70 people live with us, short-term and long-term, married and unmarried, Americans and internationals, males and females, mostly young adults, but some older. We have tried always to have a guest room available for those needing a place to stay short-term or while visiting Kansas City.

A missionary to Uzbekistan and a Korean couple lived with us for six to eight months, a missionary to China for two years, and a lady from Hong Kong for a shorter time. Individuals from Canada, South Africa, England, Europe and from all over the U.S.A. have lived with us for various lengths of time.

We have had young adults from many church, social and ethnic backgrounds. At Trinity House, however, background differences were never an issue because—1) we centered our lives in Jesus Christ, 2) based our living together on God's Word, and 3) the *koinonia* of the Holy Spirit was like oil on our relationships. Our few simple community guidelines and common household chores helped things run smoothly.

Dinner Times

One of the fond memories that people have carried with them from Trinity House has been our dinner times together. If Jane had the gift of hospitality when we got married, it was a well-kept secret. But with time, it became apparent that this was one of Jane's gifts that she used for God's glory. Typically at Trinity House we had one or two major dinners together a week.

Young adults with us often came from homes where they seldom had dinners together and no real meaningful table conversations. I would direct our dinner conversations around some biblical or theological subject, current event or life in general—engaging everyone in our conversations.

Sometimes one of them would suggest a topic. One of them told me, "When I'm married and have a family, I want my dinner times to be like yours." There is more than one way to disciple the younger generation.

Ice Storm

A classic memory of community at Trinity House happened one autumn night when I was teaching a Grace Training Center class. During the evening a rainstorm came, temperatures dropped rapidly below freezing and turned into a horrendous ice storm. When we came out of class at 10 P.M., everything was covered with ¼ inch or more of ice. What normally would be a 10-15 minute drive home became a one to two hour journey. Every inch of the way was treacherous because of the ice.

That night Trinity House was packed. Fourteen people stayed the night. A man from Germany and one from Africa came home with me. They didn't want me driving by myself. Wes Hall stayed because he was returning with Carol and it was too treacherous to travel to his apartment. One of our former renters came because she had no heat in her apartment. A Canadian married couple, who are now missionaries in Romania, were without electricity and also spent the night.

Jane put a large kettle of lentil soup on and fed everyone before bedding down. She also gave them breakfast the next morning. For these kinds of reasons Jane's reward in heaven will be great!

A number of young adults who have lived with us have proposed to their future spouse somewhere in Trinity House. Ian proposed to

The Fenimore Family With Wes - 2011

Jocelyn in our living room with Jane and I and everyone else gone for the evening. Wes Hall proposed to Carol in the house as well.

Home Group

Trinity House was a hub of activity where numerous things happened. Multiple hundreds of people have been blessed in our home for which Jane and I have always been thankful. Among activities in Trinity House, we hosted a home group for a decade led by our good friends Brian and Kellie Fenimore.

Brian and I were teachers at Grace Training Center. I taught courses related to the Word; he taught courses related to the Spirit. His classes were popular and practical, as he did "hands-on" application, not just classroom lectures.

When Jane and I returned from England, Brian and Kellie were leading a home group in their home. I didn't know Brian, but I felt from the Lord that Jane and I were to join his home group. There was one big problem—the group was closed.

Jane enrolled in one of Brian's college classes and approached him about us joining his home group. Brian said he would like to have us, but his group wanted it closed. When he did propose it, there was an uproar of objections. Members were intimidated that I was a Ph.D. scholar. Some said, "if Wes joins, I will never speak again in the group." A few men said they would no longer take a turn teaching. Bill Greenman was the only one who welcomed the idea. His sentiment was, "Let them come. Bring it on."

Initially Brian told Jane the group wanted to remain closed; in effect "no" to our request. I assured Jane, "I will talk to Brian."

I told Brian, "no is not an option." Then I played a trump card—"God told me to join your group, become friends and learn from you." This was in fact true.

Brian laughed and we joined the group. Early on Kellie saw a glint of "orneriness" in my eyes and my ability to be fun. Thereafter, she was no longer intimidated and we now have a 13-year close friendship.

Getting my power chair into their house was very difficult. After a year, we moved the home group to Trinity House. The closed group developed a revolving door policy. Students, young adults, older adults and internationals attended. In the end, I learned a great deal about prophetic and healing ministry. Also Jane and Kellie became close friends. The decade we hosted the home group and participated in leading it with the Fenimores was a delightful experience in small group ministry.

How could Jane and I foresee God's purposes when He instructed us to sell our Olathe house and to buy Trinity House, while we were many miles away in England? Admittedly, it could have been a disaster if God hadn't orchestrated the whole thing. Instead, God used Trinity House as a discipleship center, influencing young adults in Kingdom relationships, ministry, values and lifestyle.

Night and Day Prayer

Wes and Jane Adams
Two Months Before Jane's Death

22

Second Time Around

Look on my affliction and deliver me.

Psalm 119:153 ESV

Jane lived the last 24 years of her life in pain. In addition to suffering headaches and other effects of high blood pressure, failure of both kidneys, 19 months of dialysis and finally kidney transplant surgery, her furnace of affliction didn't end there.

She also suffered terribly in her feet and knees, had horrible appendix and gall bladder attacks, both inflicting intense pain before being surgically removed. She experienced outrageously high cholesterol as a side effect of kidney drugs. When taking prescribed medicine to lower her cholesterol, she experienced such a toxic liver that she became too weak to function.

In spite of the intensity of her 24 years of physical suffering, Jane continued to be a devoted wife and loving caregiver. Instead of feeling sorry for herself, she continued to think of me first.

She also affirmed her relentless faith in the goodness of God by writing these lyrics:

> *For in the furnace of much affliction*
> *I have chosen you, behold—*
> *For your iron I'll give you silver*
> *For your brass I'll give you gold.*

Transplant Declines

Beginning August 2006, Jane's blood tests revealed the start of a decline in her transplanted kidney. The creatinine in her blood (normal range .5 to 1.2) progressively increased from 1.2 to 6.1 and above, until she had only eight percent kidney function remaining.

This progressive decline happened the last four years of Jane's life. Numerous invasive procedures were done to determine why, but no disease was found. Doctors concluded her decline was the side effect of 20 years of medicine she was required to take.

During the decline, Jane and I visited her nephrologist every three months to chart her creatinine level. The creatinine increased slowly at first, but then increased by large amounts. Between each appointment, we and others prayed earnestly for healing and a good report. Time and time again we were disappointed. A few times the creatinine remained stable, but usually it increased.

Eventually it became apparent that Jane was going to need another kidney or go on dialysis again. She went on the transplant list, but this time the wait was long. Whereas the average wait for a kidney is one to two years, 12 months passed—nothing! Jane didn't even appear as a backup candidate when kidneys were available. We continued to pray for a healing miracle; but if that were not forthcoming, we prayed that an available kidney would occur for Jane in His perfect timing.

After 18 months, time was running out for Jane, so we considered a living donor. Sometimes a relative or friend will choose to donate because a person can live a healthy and normal length of life with one kidney.

Big Surprise

My sister and Jane's brother's wife were tested as possible donors. My sister was disqualified and it didn't work out for Jane's sister-in-law.

Eventually a close friend of ours, Ron Stewart, who is now on staff at IHOPKC and one of my caregivers, volunteered to donate one of his kidneys. Ron is married, and has a son and daughter who were 15 and 19 at the time. He qualified, and the double surgery date for him and Jane was scheduled towards the end of September 2010.

To everybody's surprise, on September 7, 2010, Jane received a call saying a young kidney was available and was a good match for her. Within twelve hours, she was in surgery.

Before and during Jane's surgery, 20 intercessors prayed at the hospital chapel. Most of them were still there when the surgeon came to report that the surgery had gone smoothly and everything was perfect. This was less than three weeks before Ron's surgery was scheduled as a living donor.

Recovery

Jane's post-surgery recovery progressed nicely. Her doctors mentioned several times that she had received a very good kidney and would never need another transplant. We all rejoiced at this good news. The long wait was over and future visits to the nephrologist would no longer be stressful.

After five days of post-surgery recovery in hospital isolation, Jane continued her recovery at home. We all rejoiced in the provision of this kidney that made Ron's donation no longer necessary.

For a time, Jane's immune system had to be drastically suppressed by drugs to assure her body would not reject the new organ. The drugs used to keep rejection from occurring had improved since Jane's first transplant, and everything seemed to be going normally.

One "small" concern occurred after surgery. The first blood tests revealed a substance that indicated a possible problem with the heart. Jane was thoroughly tested by a cardiologist and nothing of concern was found. Her team of four doctors concluded there was nothing to be concerned about.

Her recovery continued exceptionally well. Initially Jane's visitors were few because of her suppressed immune system, but gradually the drug dosages were reduced and more visitors were permitted. I had just begun teaching an International House of Prayer University (IHOPU) class on revival, and Jane looked forward to being in the class soon.

Maria, a precious friend of Jane's from Wamego High School days, flew in from Phoenix, enthusiastically encouraged by her husband, Jerry, to help by spending the week with Jane. It was a delightful week for Jane, Maria, and myself. The three other members of our household also enjoyed her visit. We all rejoiced at how well Jane was doing.

23

Love And Death

What therefore God has joined together,
let no man separate, until death do them part.[1]

Matthew 19:6 NASB

On Sunday evening, six weeks after her transplant, Jane's blood pressure had gone down and her pulse had gone up—dramatically. I was so alarmed, I called an ambulance and took Jane to the hospital ER. Two hours later, Jane had a severe heart attack.

When her heart monitor flat lined, oxygen and CPR were immediately given. Her heart didn't respond. After some time, the ER doctor came to where I was pacing and praying in the hallway. The spiritual atmosphere around me was heavy and so was my heart. His remarks were brief, "It looks very grim. We're doing all we can."

"Please keep trying," I responded. I couldn't give up—*love is as strong as death.*[2]

They worked on Jane for about 50 minutes, the longest 50 minutes in my life. I had seen Jane grimace in pain when the attack occurred. Would Jane rally, look at me again with her blue-green eyes and reassure my own heart she would be all right?

When the doctor appeared the second time, he said, "We've done everything we can do. She's been without oxygen long enough that, should she live, she'd be a vegetable."

"I want to see her."

He warned me, "It's not a pretty sight."

Everyone in the room looked tired and defeated. They had stopped giving CPR. They resumed so I could see for myself the futility of their effort. Each time they stopped, Jane's heart would go flat line. There was no heartbeat. None!

Final Moments

"Love is strong as death."[3] I told everyone in the room, "I want to pray."

I prayed out loud in the presence of the doctor, nurses and respiratory therapists. It was not a long prayer, but it was intense. I thanked God for His love and goodness, and asked if possible that He would work a miracle of restoration and healing and give Jane back.

As I was praying, I realized in my spirit that my prayer was not going to be answered. The awareness was real and vivid, and I knew it was a gentle "no" from the Father. When I finished praying, I asked the team to try one more time to start Jane's heart. They did, but the results were the same.

By this time the nephrologist had arrived. One by one the doctors and nurses sought to console me in my incredible loss. I appreciated their compassion, but my heart was full of pain. I wanted to be left alone with Jane. They said they would remove the equipment and the IV and then call me back.

Fortunately, I was not by myself. Kathy, who had lived with Jane and I for seven years, was present. She helped Jane in many different ways during her post-surgery recovery—tending to her needs, attending to the house, preparing food or administering the meals that were brought in by the body of Christ, and assisting me along with two other caregivers.

Kathy had gone to the ER with Jane in the ambulance and had called Santi, another of my caregivers, and Lanelle who also lived with us. Santi and Lanelle arrived almost immediately after Jane died.

My Goodbye

When the ER staff had Jane ready, Kathy, Santi, and Lanelle accompanied me into the room. I rolled alongside the bed and held her hand for a while. Then I asked Santi to adjust Jane so that I could put my face to hers.

During those moments I remembered Jane's Uncle Paul, who had a heart attack and died in the hospital, but then came back into his body. A few years before, He had told me this story:

> When my heart stopped, I left my body and could see everything that was going on. I saw the doctor speak to the nurses that there was no more they could do. I saw the doctor go out in the hall and put his arm around my wife to comfort her and say that they had done all they could do.
>
> In the meantime my spirit went to heaven. That experience was something no words could adequately describe. Heaven was so glorious! I didn't want to come back to earth. The Lord said I needed to go back for my wife's sake. Then I saw my spirit come back into my body and my heart began to beat again, with no brain damage done.[4]

"Love is as strong as death. . .unyielding as the grave."[5] Rolling my power wheelchair alongside Jane's body, I put my face next to hers. It was starting to feel cold in death. I spoke as if she could hear, "Jane, I love you dearly. You mean more to me than human words can express. Thank you for choosing to spend your life with me and loving me so well. I will miss you greatly."

I chose to believe Jane's spirit was still lingering. "Jane, I release you to the Lord and to go be with Him. You have been a faithful bride to the end!" Then by faith I added, "I'll be OK." I kissed her one last time and left the room.

My precious bride, faithfully at my side for 30 years, was swiftly released from her furnace of affliction. A long list of family, friends and people in ministry for whom Jane prayed every day suddenly lost their most faithful intercessor. Myself? My loss was incalculable! Her love had been a seal on my heart.[6] The "until-death-do-us-part" moment had come, the painful moment when the death-separation of temporal love occurs. The finality of earthly death was staring me in the face. I would never again be able to hold Jane and love her as before.

As I rolled through the ER at 2:30 A.M. that mid-October night, there was a holy hush over the place. *"The death of His godly one[s]"*[7] is truly *"precious in the sight of the LORD,"*[8] even in an ER. The nurses weren't talking. The doctor wasn't talking. Everything was silent. A lingering, holy moment gripped the entire area. The only words spoken, as I rolled out, were those of nurses and medical personnel expressing their hushed and respectful sympathy.

Clinging to Him

Jane was much more than words can describe. When I said goodbye to her, I lost what everyone else loses when his or her spouse dies. I lost the one I dearly loved and adored, the one from whom I had received such profound love. The earthly flame had flickered and died. I lost my beloved, my best friend and ministry partner, but so much more! She was my irreplaceable lover and caregiver for 30 years.

No longer would I have her at my side in bed for pillow talk, to turn me in the night; nor to get me up in the morning, dress me, prepare breakfast and help me during the day in countless ways. I loved her deeply! My loss was enormous!

I was numb as I drove home in the dark. I felt alone. As I turned my van into our sub-division and onto the driveway of Trinity House, the reality that Jane would never come home with me again hit hard. Enormous pain and loneliness descended on me. I finally went to bed at 5:30 A.M. to get less than two hours sleep, utterly exhausted, before the phone calls began.

During the first few days, my loss overwhelmed me. The sadness and emptiness I felt in Jane's absence was shocking! I knew that things were now much better for Jane. I also was painfully aware that life was going to be much more difficult for me. But I knew this was not a time for self-pity!

Since my hospital encounter with Jesus at 16, the Lord had remained faithfully at my side for five decades. Surely that would not change now. Once again, I must trust Him with all my heart and lean not on my limited understanding. This was the time, more so than ever before, to cling to Him.

Jane lived her life according to Jesus' paradigm of serving and laying one's life down for another. She had received an assignment from God, completed it and now received the reward of a life well lived. One could almost hear the pronouncement in Heaven, "Well done, my beloved and faithful daughter!"

---

[1] *The Wedding Vows; also Romans 7:1-2.*

[2] *Song of Songs 8:6 NIV*

[3] *Song of Songs 8:6 ESV*

[4] *Paul Peterson, living in California.*

[5] *Song of Songs 8:6 NIV*

[6] *Song of Songs 8:6 NIV*

[7] *Psalm 116:15 NASB*

[8] *Psalm 116:15 NASB*

> *Some who seem least important now will be the greatest then, and some who are the greatest now will be least important then.*
>
> *--Jesus*

24

True Greatness

He who humbles himself will be exalted.

Luke 14:11 NKJLV

When Jane died in a Kansas City ER, one of my caregivers, Santi, saw me verbally release her to God. At that moment, he had a vision and saw Jane being received into heaven with a great cloud of witnesses standing by.

In this life Jane didn't like being the center of attention. She didn't like the spotlight. The Holy Scriptures say numerous times in both Testaments that those who humble themselves will be exalted, and those who exalt themselves will be humbled. Jane never exalted herself; she always remained humble—a reality that was expressed in numerous ways.

But in the vision, she was now being escorted to an exalted place in heaven. Jane was taken to a great hall of honor. There she joined others who had served well in this life and were being honored for their service. Instead of being seated at the back as the most recent arrival, however, she was escorted to the front. It was her time to be exalted.

Jesus defined true greatness differently than do we. He identified greatness as related to loving, having a serving heart, and characterized by humility.

For whoever exalts himself will be humbled, and he who humbles himself will be exalted.[1]

Some who seem least important now will be the greatest then, and some who are the greatest now will be least important then.[2]

And whoever desires to be first among you, let him be your servant.[3]

Served Unselfishly

Jane had a humble and pure heart when it came to serving. It was true of our relationship, but also characterized Jane in relationship to others who needed to be served.

When Jesus taught his disciples the "lesson of the towel," He took the role of a household servant and washed His disciple's feet. He asked His disciples after washing their feet—

"'Do you understand what I have done for you?' he asked them. 'You call me "Teacher" and "Lord," and rightly so, for that is what I am. Now that I, your Lord and Teacher, have washed your feet, you also should wash one another's feet.'[4]

The enduring principle of Jesus is that we are to serve one another, no matter what our place in life. Jesus said, *"Do as I have done for you. I tell you the truth, no servant is greater than his master, nor a messenger greater than the one who sent him."[5]*

Jesus spoke of leaders in His day that loved to be shown reverence in public, had the most important seats in the synagogues and took the places of honor at banquets. In contrast, Jesus taught His disciples not to exalt themselves but humbly to serve instead. Jesus added, *"For who is greater, he who sits at the table, or he who serves? . . . I am among you as the One who serves."[6]* Jesus is greatest of all! Herein lies true greatness—voluntary serving as Jesus served.

Upside Down Kingdom

On another occasion Jesus instructed His disciples not to take the best seats at a banquet. Let someone else call you to the front, instead of pushing your way there. In His kingdom, Jesus said, *"The last will be first, and the first last."[7]*

People who live for applause and honor in this life, God says, *"Have their portion in this life."[8]* But individuals like Jane who live not for honor in this life, will have their portion in the next life.

Jesus' kingdom and teaching look upside down to the natural mind. When Mary, because of her love for Jesus, poured very expensive perfume over Him, Judas said, *"Why this waste?"*[9]

When a person lays down his/her life for another, the natural mind views it as a "waste." It is counter to the world's value system. When a gifted person like Jane chooses, because of love, not to take the position of honor but instead chooses to serve, the world says—"What a waste!"

Jesus' kingdom values are so not of this world's liking. Jesus said the person who chooses to show their love in service will be greatest in the kingdom of heaven. Jane is viewed as great in heaven because of her laid-down life.

Because of love, Jane served me as her quad husband for 30 years without complaint or bitterness. She laid down her own life, as Jesus taught, in order to help me fulfill the calling God had placed on me. Whatever I have done for Jesus and the kingdom, she was always faithfully at my side as my helpmate. Whatever righteous influence or impact my life has had on others, Jane will share the biggest half of the reward in heaven.

Jane's gifted life was laid down and unnoticed by most people. I often told Jane that her reward in heaven would be great as a result of her unselfish pouring out of her life here.

Here honor exists at best for only a few short years; in heaven great honor is being bestowed on Jane for all the ages to come! Heaven's honor is incomparably greater than her earthly sacrifice. Jane may have been at the back of the line here, but she is at the front of the line there.

Greater Honor

When Don and I wrote the study Bible, I used to remark how our wives would get the bigger reward in heaven for their labors of love unnoticed behind the scenes. This I believe now even more firmly than when I proclaimed it then, even though I said it sincerely. Jesus taught and practiced the principle—whoever desires to become great among you shall be your servant.[10]

Like Joseph, Jane was a dreamer. Among her many significant dreams were two dreams of mansions in the next life. When she described these phenomenal structures to me, I got a glimpse of the poverty of human language to describe heaven's indescribable glory. I knew the dreams referred to the exceptional honor that Jane would have in the age to come.

A much-loved spiritual son of ours was in Korea when Jane died. When John learned about her death, he was greatly saddened and asked the Lord, "Why now?" The only answer he sensed from the Lord was, "She is with the apostles."

As a result of John hearing and Santi seeing what was going on in the spiritual realm, I could see Jane—humble and unassuming—being ushered to the front of the line to a place made for her in the company of those who will be eternally great in God's kingdom.

---

[1] Luke 14:11 NKJV

[2] Luke 13:30 NLT

[3] Matthew 20:27

[4] John 13:12-13 NIV

[5] John 13:15-16 NIV

[6] Luke 22:27 NKJV

[7] Matthew 20:16 ESV

[8] Psalm 17:14 NKJV

[9] Matthew 26:8; cf. John 12:4-7

[10] Mark 10:43 NKJV

25

Omega Reflections

How precious to me are your thoughts, O God!
How vast is the sum of them!

Psalm 139:17 NIV

H ere are a few final reflections about Jane, mostly by her best friend, Kellie Fenimore, from emails with me after Jane's death. Kellie serves me as a part-time secretary/bookkeeper, is a close friend and daughter to me, as well as one of my three godly caregivers.

She wrote me the following on a day when I was intensely missing Jane:

Wes, you lost someone who was so dear, kind, sweet, loving, who covered you well, who made so much possible for you, the one who made your heart leap. She was faithful, committed, ever-attending, compassionate, someone who always had you and your best interest in her thoughts. The list can go on and on and on! Of course you miss her and this is difficult.

The only thing better than Jane that you have had is the Lord. All the things she was to you, He was the giver of it all in the first place. He formed and molded her, and how Jane cooperated with Him in her godly character development. I was blessed to be her friend and saw these things and so much more.

I miss her too. I was looking at the picture of the two of you in your living room when Ian and Jocelyn were over, and I started to cry. She was so wonderful and I valued her opinion of me more than ANY other friend I have ever had. So, if I get saddened and wish she were still here and miss her encouraging words to me that so often melted my heart, I can't imagine what you are going through.

I am SO proud of how you are walking this out with the Lord! Your heart is continuing to stay engaged towards Him and that is the best thing you can do. He will never leave you nor forsake you, never! He will strengthen you according to His Word as He has done since you were young!

You are a blessed man! You have accomplished amazing things in your life because of God and I am blessed to be able to glean things from you, which I hold so dear to my heart! I love you dear Wes. I am here for you anytime you need an ear, a hug or to feel loved, thought of, valued and appreciated! Thank you for blessing Brian's and my life, and our children's!!!!!!!! Besides, you also have Carol and Wes. You are SO loved!-Kellie

On another day Kellie wrote me these words of encouragement:

Was pondering and thinking about Jane a lot this morning. My heart misses her so much—her smile, laughter, sense of humor, her resolved and determined heart for the Lord to walk in righteousness.

Since seeing so much more of your life, I have grown to love Jane even more. I realize, as you talk about her, how much more I can still learn from her and grow in my own character, purity and heart for the things of God! She was such an amazing lady, such an amazing woman of God. Her death wasn't a death that has no fruit or influence on others. There is SO much to glean and learn from your lives together, and from her life and heart. Thirty years together—wow!

That is such a long time to do all that she did for you and keep her heart from growing bitter, angry and closing it off to you and the Lord. AMAZING! So many (most) women wouldn't last for long and definitely wouldn't last without wanting to fulfill their own lives.

I definitely believe your desire to write a book about Jane is SO worthwhile, so worth the effort and so worth going through the pain of recalling all the memories in her absence; there will be healing and joy for you in writing and facing the pain.

Writing will make you stronger in many ways and enable you to see more clearly the goodness of God in your life and His love for you. I want to learn more and partake of the fruit of Jane's life. What a servant she was and filled with SO much love, grounded in love.

I hope this is ok to share because I don't want to make you sad. Her life was not in vain, and the testimony of her life and death has a lot to offer to those who will hear. I love you dear Wes!!! - Kellie

A good friend and former parishioner in Olathe, Ken Coumerilh, wrote these words of reflection: "Indeed Jane was special, a wonderful friend, brilliant, full of joy always, mischievous, delightful sense of humor, a treasure among people I have known in my life. Did I say she could run fast? I am looking forward very much to seeing her again."

Two people have had subsequent glimpses of her. Kellie had an amazing dream about Jane four months after her death. As a context, Jane longed in this life to be able to worship God with the same freedom she felt in her spirit. Hence the significance of Kellie's dream.

I was sitting on the floor against the big couch in Wes' living room. Wes was in between the couch and the green chair that he, Jane and his mother liked. There were two ladies in the room. I didn't recognize them. One was sitting to my right and the other was to my left by the piano. We were all looking towards the fireplace and it was as if we were reminiscing about Jane. The room was "ALIVE—with the presence of the Lord" in the sense that it felt as if we were in another place. There was a tangible presence of the Lord in the room with us.

At some point Jane just "appeared" to the left of the fireplace. She was a bit taller and slimmer. Her hair was a bit longer, still gray but not gray at the same time (don't quite know how to explain). She was SO full of life, fully ALIVE! Her eyes were bright and full of joy—alive. Her countenance was peaceful, bright and shiny alive. Her beauty was so amazing, so different than our human bodies. Wes, Jane was SO beautiful!!!

There was a continual smile on her face. When she appeared, she was dancing freely in worship to the Lord.

There was such freedom, grace and joy in her dancing. Her steps on the floor were so light and easy (not at all like how she walked with the pain in her feet here). She never even seemed to notice that we were watching her. She was so intent on the Lord, so focused on Him that all she could see was Him. She was in such a place of adoration before her Lord, so free and full of joy, gazing at Him.

The room was full of LIGHT from the presence of the Lord. It was as if a part of heaven opened up and dropped into Wes' living room for a brief time. The room was SO alive and full of LIFE. We were part of another place or another place entered our space—hard to explain. I suppose it was the Lord's tangible presence so close, so dense. It was similar to my experience when standing before the Lord, but not quite the same.

I watched her for a while and then grabbed the woman next to me by both shoulders and asked her, "Are you seeing what I am?" She said yes. Wes was SO at peace. As Jane danced, I could literally feel each step she took as it gently landed on the floor. I took the lady by the shoulders again and asked her, "Can you feel it?" We continued to watch her for some time. Then she was gone. The experience left such a peace and joy, it touched all of us to the very depth of our being.

Sung Jin, one of our Korean friends and spiritual offspring in Seattle, loved Jane dearly. When he first heard the news of her departure, his heart was broken. He tried to write an email to me but just couldn't put his words together. So he decided to pray.

While he was praying, he suddenly had a clear vision of Jane, singing praise to God. Here is his description:

I had a side-view of her, yet, it was such an overwhelmingly glorious sight that human words just cannot describe. Her face shining like the sun, full of perfect peace, inexpressibly joyful and she was so pure and lovely...beyond this world.

I just wish I could describe the vision better. I was so completely captured by the amazing vision of Jane that I was lost in time for a while. Then suddenly supernatural joy flooded into my heart as God was letting me see the current status of Jane in heaven, how she is filled with peace and joy in God's presence.

Kellie's dream and Sung Jin's vision provide a fitting conclusion for my portrait of Jane's life poured out because of love. Like the eternal Bride, Jane is enthralled with the heavenly Bridegroom now and pouring out her love and worship on Him—forever!

Jane Worshipping In 1986

There is a tenacious flame of love that will never die and a Bride that will live forever.

The Bible ends its centuries-long redemptive story with a wedding invitation: "The Spirit and the Bride say, 'Come!'"

Revelation 22:17

26

A Bride Forever

Let us rejoice and be glad and give the glory to Him. . .
His bride has made herself ready

Revelation 19:7 NASB

Part of the sting of death, on earth, is the death of temporal love. When my bride died, she was no longer there to love. The death of love on a marital level leaves an indescribable empty space and ache that is deep and painful.

May 15th, Jane's birthday in 2011, was my first one without her. The 15th that year also marked my return as a faculty member to a university graduation ceremony. I had two revelatory moments towards its end. Both brought tears to my eyes, one because of great joy and the other because of great sadness.

In a special kiss from God, I saw how He had brought me full circle back to a university setting, my first faculty procession since May 1982 when I was honored as university *Teacher of the Year.* The goodness of the Lord in bringing me currently into an international setting where 24/7 worship and prayer is foundational made my heart very happy and grateful.

Right behind this was a somber realization. Jane who had been at my side in all previous ministry and academic moments since 1981 was not there and wouldn't ever be again. The emptiness and loss I felt that moment in Jane's absence was shocking!

Only God can fill the vacuum. In Him there is a living flame of love that will never die and a Bride that will live forever.

Created for Love

A foremost reason God created us in His image was for love. The very capacity to love is from Him. *"We love Him because He first loved us."*[1]

The "why" behind creation and redemption is this: the Father wanted to have a family for himself (many children) and an eternal companion for Jesus (a Bride), one who would be equally yoked with the God-man in love.

God is not cold and emotionless; God is love and His love is filled with desire and affection. Love finds pleasure in others. God, who has everything and needs nothing, still has desire because He is love. God loves—not out of need, but from the fountainhead of overflowing desire for those whom He has created. The measure of the Father's affection for His Son, Jesus, is the measure of His affection for all His sons and daughters. Only His love can fully satisfy our heart's desire for love and intimacy.

Because we were created for love, deep within every person is the need to be loved and to love. The human need to receive and give love originates with God. We cannot be whole until we are confident in God's love for us and are able to respond wholeheartedly with love for Him.

Earthly love has two dimensions—vertical and horizontal. Vertical love is the fulfillment of what Jesus called the first and greatest commandment, namely to love God with abandonment—all our heart, soul, mind and strength.[2] Loving God with all our being is our greatest charge and privilege from God.

God also created us to love on a horizontal plane. Jesus said the second greatest commandment is to love others as we love ourselves.[3] The highest expression of horizontal love is covenantal, like marriage-love between a husband and wife, itself a picture of the love relationship God designs for our lives with Him and His Son.

Love is the greatest virtue. There are three spiritual dynamics that are supremely important in life—*"faith, hope and love. But the greatest of these is love."*[4] God's love is the ultimate revelation of our worth and dignity.

Multiple times Paul emphasized the primacy of love. He prayed for us to be rooted and grounded in love.[5] Only when we *"grasp how wide and long and high and deep is the love of Christ that surpasses knowledge,"*[6] do we become a candidate to *"be filled with all the fullness of God."*[7]

Our endless challenge is to grow in the width, length, height and depth of Christ's love. Love is the key for entering into God's heart and enjoying Him forever. The anointing to love God is the highest anointing of all, and in turn enables us to love others as we love ourselves. Paul writes, *"I pray that your love may abound still more and more."*[8]

Bridal Love

The Bible begins[9] and ends[10] with a wedding. In this life, God intends amorous love between a man and a woman to move toward a wedding and permanent covenant partnership, until dissolved by death. Likewise, the love relationship between Christ and His Church is destined to move toward a wedding and permanent covenant partnership, one that will never be dissolved by death.

Bridal love is covenant love. Revelation of God's plan for a bride, along with marriage and family, are at the heart of biblical redemption and the meaning of biblical covenant.

God is preparing for His Son a Bride who will be eternally yoked in covenant love with Him. The Father's design is that we love the Son with the same love that He has for Him.[11]

The Bible reveals we are the delight of God's eyes. His eyes roam to and fro throughout the earth, looking for those whose hearts are fully His.[12] In so doing, the Father is looking for a loving and faithful Bride for His Son.

Bridal love is the language of active intimacy. A pure bride loves the bridegroom with a single-hearted devotion, just as the bridegroom pours out his love for the bride. The Bride that God is preparing for His Son will be one who is wholehearted in love, and who expresses affection lavishly for the Bridegroom in worship, loyalty, and faithfulness.

This was one of Jane's most commendable virtues, her wholehearted love for me and her complete faithfulness as my wife. This is a picture of Christ and the Church.[13]

Jesus fulfills the function of Bridegroom in His heart's affection for His redeemed beloved in the earth. He is essentially a Bridegroom who feels, thinks, and acts as a bridegroom would towards a bride. From creation the Father was committed to give Jesus a bride as His inheritance, and Jesus was committed to purchase the Bride with His own blood on the cross.

Jesus taught two parables comparing the Kingdom to a wedding. Both of these parables were in the final week of His life—one spoken publically,[14] and the other spoken privately.[15] In the second marriage parable, Jesus privately exhorted His disciples not to neglect their affection and intimacy with Him as an intrinsic part of being ready for their Bridegroom.[16]

When we behold the glory of God in Jesus' face and gaze upon His beauty, we are transformed from glory to glory into His likeness.[17] By focusing on Jesus, our fixed gaze awakens bridal love in our heart for Him and transforms us into a partner of beauty. Our Bridegroom loves us, places His seal on our heart and thereby marks us as His beloved, and then teaches us how to love Him in return.

Faithful and True

Jesus' first miracle was turning water into wine at a wedding. When the miracle-wine was served to the wedding guests, the master commented to the bridegroom, *"You have saved the best till now [last]."*[18] Likewise, God is saving the "best" wine of the Spirit for the end time of history when His power and revelation are released in the Church in greatest measure as part of the Bride's preparation for the wedding of the Lamb.[19]

John Hwang, a Korean businessman from Seattle whom Jane and I have known as a spiritual son for over 20 years, remarked ten days after Jane's death: "Your union with Jane was one so rare on the earth, that it is full of characteristics reflecting the eternal union of the Church with her Bridegroom."

If this is true, what was Jane's most remarkable feature? Was it her amazing intelligence or wisdom? Was it her giftedness? Was it her pure life and noble character? Was it her amazing capacity to serve? All of these characteristics are commendable virtues and all were true of her. But her most remarkable feature was her tenacious love and unwavering faithfulness as a bride.

Because of love, Jane was preeminently faithful and true— the very virtue that Jesus is looking for in His Bride. At His second coming, Jesus will be called *"Faithful and True."*[20] Likewise, the eternal Bride—as she is transformed from glory to glory into His likeness—will be "faithful and true," motivated by the living flame of love!

When the marriage of the Lamb occurs, the Bride will have made herself ready.[21] Then John hears a voice saying, *"Come, I will show you the Bride, the wife of the Lamb."*[22]

Radiant Bride

The Bible not only *begins* with a perfect bridegroom (Adam) and a radiant bride (Eve) being joined as one in marriage, the Bible also *ends* with a wedding—the marriage of Jesus, the perfect Bridegroom, and His radiant Bride.

The final description of the cherished redeemed at the end of the age is as Jesus' glorious Bride. Isaiah saw the prominence of the bridal paradigm in the end time when he prophesied that God's people will be called *"Hephzibah."* The literal translation of this Hebrew word is: *"My delight is in her."*[23] Then, Isaiah added: *"As the bridegroom rejoices over the bride, so shall your God rejoice over you."*[24]

Jesus' words in John 14-17 are full of revelation of His love for His beloved disciples. He reminded them and us, *"These things I have spoken to you, that My joy may remain in you, and that your joy may be full."*[25]

John later sees *"in the Spirit"* the intense full-joy moment when Jesus will be joined with His Bride forever. He records: *"'Let us be glad and rejoice and give Him glory, for the marriage of the Lamb has come, and His wife has made herself ready.' And he said to me, 'These are the true sayings of God.'"*[26]

Love's living flame in the heart of the Bridegroom for the Bride, and in the heart of the Bride for the Bridegroom, is an all-consuming fire that will continue to burn throughout eternity. Moreover, the Bride will continue to grow in the width and length, height and depth of Christ's love throughout the endless ages to come.

Jesus is coming for a pure and transformed Bride, full of joy, radiant with the light of His glory and glowing with surpassing love! God is not finished with His Bride yet!

The Bride will never find transformation in human wisdom, church programs or self-help gimmicks! The church will not make the journey to full maturity and readiness[27] without learning to live in intimacy with Christ, in oneness with the Holy Spirit and in agreement with the core values of God's kingdom.

When Jesus appears, the prepared Bride will be like the five virgins, ready for His arrival.[28] The prepared Bride will be *"a glorious church, not having spot or wrinkle or any such thing, but . . . holy and without blemish"*[29]—clothed in the true beauty of holiness. She will be in perfect agreement with the Spirit's voice preceding Jesus' return.[30]

The Bible concludes by further describing the Bride's joy at the marriage and in the bridal city.[31] Bonded with the Bridegroom in love, the Bride will rule and reign at Jesus' side forever—as a queen would be at the side of a king.

Invitation

The Bible ends its centuries-long redemptive story with a wedding invitation: *"The Spirit and the Bride say, 'Come.'"*[32]

> *There's going to be a wedding,*
> *People get ready!*[33]

The prophet Isaiah foresees the ultimate moment: *"Your eyes will see the King in His beauty."*[34]

The lyrics from two contemporary songs express the growing anticipation in the heart of the Bride for the coming wedding:

> *There's gonna be a wedding,*
> *It's the reason that I'm living,*
> *to marry the Lamb!*
> —Tim Reimherr (IHOPKC)

> *I see You there hanging on a tree*
> *And then You rose again for me*
> *Now You are sitting on Your heavenly throne*
> *Soon we will be coming home*
> *You're beautiful, You're beautiful*

> *When we arrive at eternity's shore*
> *Where death is just a memory and tears are no more*

We'll enter in as the wedding bells ring
Your bride will come together and we'll sing
[Jesus] You're beautiful!
                    —Phil Wickham

We know in part and see in part now; we'll see face to face then! Tenacious love is necessary now! Fullness of love then! The flame of love will burn more brightly then than now! The Bridegroom who is *"Faithful and True,"* the perfection of love and beauty, will be united with a Bride who is faithful and true, transformed into His likeness—to His honor, glory and praise forever and forever! Amen!

---

[1] *1 John 4:19 NKJV*

[2] *Matthew 22:37-38*

[3] *Matthew 22:39-40*

[4] *1 Corinthians 13:13 NIV*

[5] *Ephesians 3:17*

[6] *Ephesians 3:19 NIV (1984)*

[7] *Ephesians 3:19 NKJV*

[8] *Philippians 1:9 NKJV*

[9] *Adam & Eve; Genesis 2:18, 21-24*

[10] *Revelation 19:7; 21:1—22:21*

[11] *John 17:26*

[12] *2 Chronicles 16:9*

[13] *Ephesians 5:22-32*

[14] *Matthew 22:1-14*

[15] *Matthew 25:1-13*

[16] *Matthew 25:1-13*

[17] *2 Corinthians 3:18*

[18] *John 2:9-10 NIV*

[19] *cf. Joel 2:28-29; Revelation 19:7-9*

[20] *Revelation 19:11*

[21] *Revelation 19:7*

[22] *Revelation 21:9 ESV*

[23] *Isaiah 62:4*

[24] *Isaiah 62:5 ESV*

[25] *John 15:11 NKJV*

[26] *Revelation 19:7, 9 NKJV*

[27] *Ephesians 4:13*

[28] Matthew 25:1-13

[29] Ephesians 5:27 NKJV

[30] Revelation 22:12-15, 17

[31] Revelation 19, 21-22

[32] Revelation 22:17

[33] Lyrics by Misty Edwards, IHOPKC

[34] Isaiah 33:17 NKJV

About the Author

John Wesley ("Wes") Adams, B.A., M.A., M.Div., Ph.D., is a professor, scholar, minister, author and public speaker. He has written numerous articles (for magazines and journals), Bible commentaries and books on a variety of subjects. He is contributing author and associate editor of the *Fire Bible*, a study Bible published in over 40 languages and distributed on six continents. He continues to teach a few courses at the university level.

Dr. Adams' four earned degrees are from three academic institutions of higher learning. The degrees were all obtained with honors and all studies were done in residence (on site, not online)—

B.A., Southern Nazarene University (*Cum Laude*)

M.A., Southern Nazarene University (Summa Cum Laude)

> *M.A. Thesis: "The Unresolved Problems of the Epistle to the Hebrews & Their Relation to the Authenticity of Its Canonical Authority"*

M.Div., Nazarene Theological Seminary (*Magna Cum Laude*)

Ph.D., Baylor University (*Summa Cum Laude*)

> *Ph.D. Dissertation: "The Teaching Role in the New Testament: Its Nature and Scope As a Function of the Developing Church"*

The author's favorite activity (other than ministry) is travel. He and his wife Jane (30 years married before her death) traveled to Brazil (7 weeks), Guatemala, seven European nations, England (4 summers; living there 2 years plus), Scotland, Wales, Canada and 40 of our 50 states in the USA.

In May 2016, Dr. Adams completed 58 years as a quadriplegic, having suffering a spinal cord injury at age 16 in an auto accident. He has been active and healthy since his discharge from a physical rehabilitation center in November 1959. He has never once been hospitalized during the subsequent five plus decades. He attributes his health and longevity as a quadriplegic first to the life-giving and life-sustaining power of God and in His word, then to lifestyle wisdom, disciplined heath habits, good caregivers, a righteous heritage and finally good family genes.

Adams' book, *Tenacious Love,* is about his life and especially that of his wife, Jane. Additional copies of the book may be purchased from Forerunner Book Store at IHOPKC.ORG or from amazon.com

Other Books by John Wesley Adams
(available on Amazon.com)

Wholeness Is Possible: A Paralytic Speaks Out (Trinity House Press, 2015)

Revival: It's Present Relevance & Coming Role at the End of the Age, by John Wesley Adams & Rhonda Hughey (Fusion Ministries, 2010)

God, Fire & Revival, by John Wesley Adams and Owen Murphy (Trinity House press, 2016)

The Fire Bible, by Donald C. Stamps and John Wesley Adams (Hendrickson Publishers, 1992, 2010)

"Ephesians" and "Hebrews" Commentaries, by John Wesley Adams in *Life in the Spirit New Testament Commentary.* Editors: French L. Arrington and Roger Stronstad (Zondervan, 2003; order on CBD or Amazon.com)

41469010R00118

cry. She was so wonderful and I valued her opinion of me more than ANY other friend I have ever had. So, if I get saddened and wish she were still here and miss her encouraging words to me that so often melted my heart, I can't imagine what you are going through.

I am SO proud of how you are walking this out with the Lord! Your heart is continuing to stay engaged towards Him and that is the best thing you can do. He will never leave you nor forsake you, never! He will strengthen you according to His Word as He has done since you were young!

You are a blessed man! You have accomplished amazing things in your life because of God and I am blessed to be able to glean things from you, which I hold so dear to my heart! I love you dear Wes. I am here for you anytime you need an ear, a hug or to feel loved, thought of, valued and appreciated! Thank you for blessing Brian's and my life, and our children's!!!!!!!! Besides, you also have Carol and Wes. You are SO loved!-Kellie

On another day Kellie wrote me these words of encouragement:

Was pondering and thinking about Jane a lot this morning. My heart misses her so much—her smile, laughter, sense of humor, her resolved and determined heart for the Lord to walk in righteousness.

Since seeing so much more of your life, I have grown to love Jane even more. I realize, as you talk about her, how much more I can still learn from her and grow in my own character, purity and heart for the things of God! She was such an amazing lady, such an amazing woman of God. Her death wasn't a death that has no fruit or influence on others. There is SO much to glean and learn from your lives together, and from her life and heart. Thirty years together—wow!

That is such a long time to do all that she did for you and keep her heart from growing bitter, angry and closing it off to you and the Lord. AMAZING! So many (most) women wouldn't last for long and definitely wouldn't last without wanting to fulfill their own lives.

I definitely believe your desire to write a book about Jane is SO worthwhile, so worth the effort and so worth going through the

25

Omega Reflections

How precious to me are your thoughts, O God!
How vast is the sum of them!

Psalm 139:17 NIV

Here are a few final reflections about Jane, mostly by her best friend, Kellie Fenimore, from emails with me after Jane's death. Kellie serves me as a part-time secretary/bookkeeper, is a close friend and daughter to me, as well as one of my three godly caregivers.

She wrote me the following on a day when I was intensely missing Jane:

Wes, you lost someone who was so dear, kind, sweet, loving, who covered you well, who made so much possible for you, the one who made your heart leap. She was faithful, committed, ever-attending, compassionate, someone who always had you and your best interest in her thoughts. The list can go on and on and on! Of course you miss her and this is difficult.

The only thing better than Jane that you have had is the Lord. All the things she was to you, He was the giver of it all in the first place. He formed and molded her, and how Jane cooperated with Him in her godly character development. I was blessed to be her friend and saw these things and so much more.

I miss her too. I was looking at the picture of the two of you in your living room when Ian and Jocelyn were over, and I started to